A Beginner's Guide to
SUCCULENT GARDENING

A Step-by-Step Guide to Growing
Beautiful & Long-Lasting Succulents

TAKU FURUYA

TUTTLE Publishing

Tokyo | Rutland, Vermont | Singapore

Contents

Let the Illustrations and Photos Show You How to Grow and Enjoy Succulents!

Information Included for Each Plant
Characteristics/Points to Check when Buying/Soil Composition/
Fertilizer/How to Transplant/How to Propagate/Key Points for
Growing/Cultivation Calendar/Succulent Advice Q & A

Preface

Succulents have grown in popularity year by year, and that's not surprising. They're easy to care for, tenacious and interesting to look at. Full of wonders unlike any other plant, succulents can really pique our curiosity.

Succulents evolved in dry regions with little rainfall, branching off into many diverse varieties. Their harsh native environments forced them to store water inside themselves. You might say that their charming, plump leaves, stems, and roots are the product of their accumulated survival skills. Because they seem so adaptable and self-sufficient, some people tend to think that succulents don't need water or attention. But easy as they are to grow and care for, they're still living organisms, with needs that must be met in order for these captivating plants to thrive.

This book was written for novices who want to try growing a succulent or two. I've selected 21 popular varieties, and have explained the basics of caring for them in a way that's easy to understand, with plenty of illustrations and photos to help guide you.

"How should I water my plants?" "What kind of soil should I choose?" "Where should I keep my plants?" Even these most basic of questions will be explained as thoroughly as possible. With this book, you'll have the fundamentals you need for growing beautiful, healthy succulents.

And if, because of this book, you'll be growing and enjoying succulents for years to come, there will be no greater joy for me as an author.

— Taku Furuya

How to Use this Book

Explaining Succulent Cultivation from the Most Basic of Level

This book is an introductory guide for those who want to start growing succulent plants. The information on how to grow and maintain these plants is compiled in a 4-page spread for each type of succulent included in this book. I have structured the book so the information on these spreads is complete, and you will have all the knowledge you need to grow any and all of the included varieties.

The information on potting soil composition, the points to remember when buying, and the annual calendar that come with each variety make this book a useful tool as early as the shopping stage.

I have divided the succulent varieties into three types based on their growing periods:

Spring/Fall Types—Grow the most during spring and fall. Growth slows during summer.
Spring/Summer/Fall Types—Grow throughout spring, summer, and fall. Growth slows during winter.
Fall/Winter/Spring Types— Grow throughout fall, winter, and spring, but is weak to ice forming at freezing temperatures. Dormant during summer.

The "Fundamentals for Growing Succulents" section at the end of the book covers the most basic information that is shared by all varieties, and it also acts to supplement the pages for each variety. If you scan this section first, you'll have a good preliminary base for starting your adventure with succulents.

How to Read the Symbols in this Book

Level of Difficulty

 Indicated by the number of ☆'s.
☆ Easy
☆☆ Standard
☆☆☆ Difficult

Flowering

 Indicates the season when the flowers bloom. The flowering periods are sorted into spring, fall, and winter. The number of months is also displayed.

Native Region

 Displayed on a world map. The region is the area marked in red.

Information about points to check when buying, potting soil composition, transplanting, and propagating are shown with illustrations.

The cultivation calendar shows the watering, placement and sunlight, and actions required for every season.

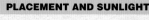

WATERING	PLACEMENT AND SUNLIGHT	ACTIONS

Lots of water | Water less frequently | Indoors, in the sun | In the sun | In partial shade | Transplanting | Propagating from a leaf cutting | Propagating from a stem cutting

For each variety, I will introduce other plants of the same genus. Challenge yourself to cultivate more difficult varieties as well.

[Example] Members of the Echeveria genus

Deciding how to decorate with succulents is part of the fun of growing them! Try setting or hanging succulents in your own homemade containers. Even with smaller plants, this is a great way to add personality to your living space.

Add succulents to small, empty places to create a stylish space. During seasons when succulents can thrive in the shade, they make the perfect accent for any room.

Everyday pleasure in a succulent plant lies in its leaves, but of course we're especially happy when the flowers bloom. The flowers that bloom only once a year are a vibrant and beautiful surprise.

Spring/Fall
Types

Echeveria rosularis / E. elegans

Characteristics of *E. rosularis* and *E. elegans*

Plants of the *Echeveria* genus are popular among succulents for their abundance of varieties and colors and for the rosette shape formed by their leaves. If *E. rosularis* and *E. elegans* are exposed to plenty of sunlight during fall and winter, the pigment in the leaves becomes more concentrated with the arrival of cold temperatures, and the plant becomes vividly beautiful.

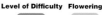

Level of Difficulty	Flowering	Native Region
★	Winter/ Spring	
Easy	Nov.–Dec. Apr.–May	Central America

Points to Check when Buying

The plant should form a compact rosette shape with a low height and little space between the leaves. The leaves should be full and plump.

The plant should not be etiolated.

The leaves should not be discolored.

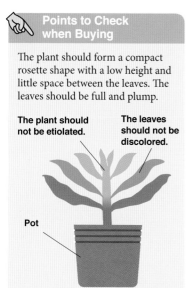

Pot

Soil Composition

Mix 5 parts small-grain Akadama, 3 parts Kanuma soil, and 2 parts mulch for a ratio that has good drainage, water retention, and breathability. Add a layer of gravel like large-grain Akadama or pumice to the bottom of the pot.

Sprinkle in an appropriate amount of granular fertilizer. You can also use liquid fertilizer.

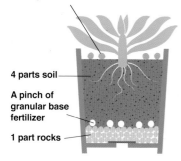

4 parts soil

A pinch of granular base fertilizer

1 part rocks

Fertilizer

When you transplant a succulent, add a layer of granular base fertilizer on top of the layer of gravel.

How to Transplant

First, pull out the plant and check it over. Remove any darkened roots and massage out the old soil. Spread the roots apart, taking care not to damage them, and add in the fresh soil mix.

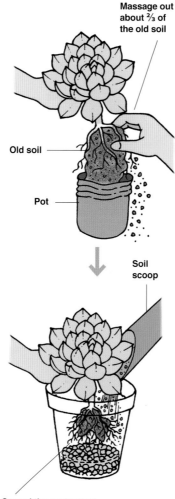

Massage out about ⅔ of the old soil

Old soil

Pot

Soil scoop

Spread the roots apart

Pour in the slightly dampened new soil. When you have finished transplanting, lightly tap the pot to level the soil and place the plant in partial shade to take root.

How to Propagate

In spring and fall, you can take leaf cuttings and stem cuttings. To propagate from a leaf cutting, simply remove the whole leaf from the stem and place it on top of a previously prepared pot of soil to let a new plant take root and sprout. To propagate from a stem cutting, cut off a branch from the main stem, let the cut end dry, and insert the cutting into the soil.

Leaf Cutting

Place the leaf you removed from the succulent stem on the surface of dampened soil, and after about 10 days the leaf will begin to take root and sprout. When your new plant has grown 4 or 5 leaves, pull it from the soil, taking care not to injure the roots, and transplant it.

Stem Cutting

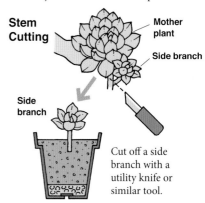

Mother plant

Side branch

Side branch

Cut off a side branch with a utility knife or similar tool.

Let the cut end of the branch dry out for 4–5 days, and then insert the branch into soil. During the first half month until the plant takes root, keep the soil constantly damp and leave the plant in partial shade. After the plant has taken root, you can care for it as usual.

9

Key Points for Growing *E. rosularis* and *E. elegans*

If you expose your plant to enough sunlight during the spring and fall periods of growth, it will grow with its leaves packed tightly together. You usually keep these plants dry under the eaves, but if you occasionally set one out and expose it to the rain, it won't be an issue. These are robust plants, but long spells of rain or overwatering will cause root rot. In summer, move your plant into partial shade and water it less frequently. On winter days that are cold enough for ice to form, move the plant into a sunny area indoors to prevent freezing.

Cultivation Calendar

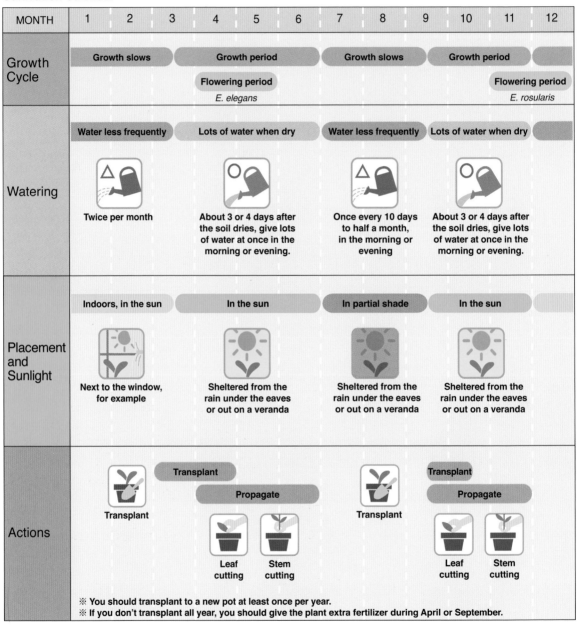

MONTH	1	2	3	4	5	6	7	8	9	10	11	12
Growth Cycle	Growth slows			Growth period			Growth slows			Growth period		
				Flowering period *E. elegans*							Flowering period *E. rosularis*	
Watering	Water less frequently			Lots of water when dry			Water less frequently			Lots of water when dry		
	Twice per month			About 3 or 4 days after the soil dries, give lots of water at once in the morning or evening.			Once every 10 days to half a month, in the morning or evening			About 3 or 4 days after the soil dries, give lots of water at once in the morning or evening.		
Placement and Sunlight	Indoors, in the sun			In the sun			In partial shade			In the sun		
	Next to the window, for example			Sheltered from the rain under the eaves or out on a veranda			Sheltered from the rain under the eaves or out on a veranda			Sheltered from the rain under the eaves or out on a veranda		
Actions	Transplant	Transplant					Transplant	Transplant				
			Propagate						Propagate			
				Leaf cutting / Stem cutting						Leaf cutting / Stem cutting		

※ You should transplant to a new pot at least once per year.
※ If you don't transplant all year, you should give the plant extra fertilizer during April or September.

Succulent Advice Q&A

Q When I watered my succulent on a hot day, it started drooping!

A Move the plant to a cool place in partial shade and refrain from watering it. Then, check on it to see if it recovers. Watering plants during the day will leave the soil soggy and full of hot water, inviting root rot. Remember to always give water in the early morning or evening.

The word "rosette" refers to a double-flowered rose. *Echeveria* plants are a representative of this shape.

E. rosularis

E. elegans

Good seedlings are short in height and have tightly packed leaves, as pictured.

Members of the *Echeveria* Genus

E. "Momotarou"

E. agavoides "Red Ebony"

E. runyonii "Topsy Turvy"

E. variegata "Hanaikada"

E. laui *Sensitive to the heat and high humidity of summer

E. affinis

Spring/Fall
Types

Graptopetalum "Francesco Baldi"

Characteristics of G. "Francesco Baldi"

Graptopetalum varieties that have been crossbred with genera like *Echeveria* or *Sedum* are quite popular. Francesco Baldi is one such hybrid. The thick leaves of Francesco Baldi form narrow elliptical shapes, and as the plant grows, its stem gradually lengthens. This plant is robust and easy to grow, and can even survive through spells of rain during its growing season; however, if it appears the rain will continue for a while, you should move the plant under the eaves.

Level of Difficulty	Flowering	Native Region
★	Spring	
Easy	Apr.–May	Central and South Africa

Avoid buying seedlings that have a long stem and a lot of space between the leaves. These plants have stretched out due to a lack of sunlight.

The plant should not be etiolated.

The leaves should not be discolored.

Pot

Soil Composition

Mix 5 parts small-grain Akadama, 3 parts Kanuma soil, and 2 parts mulch for a ratio that has good drainage, water retention, and breathability. Add a layer of gravel like large-grain Akadama or pumice to the bottom of the pot.

Sprinkle in an appropriate amount of granular fertilizer. You can also use liquid fertilizer.

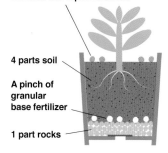

4 parts soil

A pinch of granular base fertilizer

1 part rocks

Fertilizer

When you transplant a succulent, add a layer of granular base fertilizer on top of the layer of gravel.

How to Transplant

Remove the plant from its container and move it to a sturdy pot. Remove any darkened roots, as this is a sign they are rotten. Massage out the old soil from the roots and throw it away as well. Then, add in the fresh soil mix.

Old soil

Pot

Massage out about ⅔ of the old soil

Soil scoop

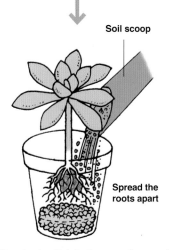

Spread the roots apart

Pour in the slightly dampened new soil. When you have finished transplanting, lightly tap the pot to level the soil and place the plant in partial shade to take root.

How to Propagate

You can propagate these succulents from leaf cuttings. Simply lay a leaf on the surface of a pot of soil for a new plant to take root and sprout. For stems that have stretched too long, cut the area under where the leaves attach and insert that stem cutting into soil.

Leaf Cutting

Place the leaf you removed from the succulent stem on the surface of dampened soil, and after about 10 days the leaf will begin to take root and sprout. When your new plant has grown 4 or 5 leaves, pull it from the soil, taking care not to injure the roots, and transplant it.

Stem Cutting

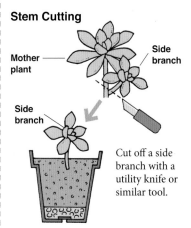

Mother plant

Side branch

Side branch

Cut off a side branch with a utility knife or similar tool.

Let the cut end of the branch dry out for 4–5 days, and then insert the branch into soil. During the first half month until the plant takes root, keep the soil constantly damp and leave the plant in partial shade. After the plant has taken root, you can care for it as usual.

Key Points for Growing G. "Francesco Baldi"

This species is very robust and can be easily propagated. During its growing season, place your succulent in a sunny place outside and expose it to direct sunlight. When the top soil gets dry, wait about 3–4 days, and then give the plant lots of water until it streams out of the hole in the bottom of the pot. This replaces the air in the soil inside the pot and is good for the roots. However, be careful not to water the plant too much or place it in an area with poor ventilation, as this can cause root rot from fungus.

Cultivation Calendar

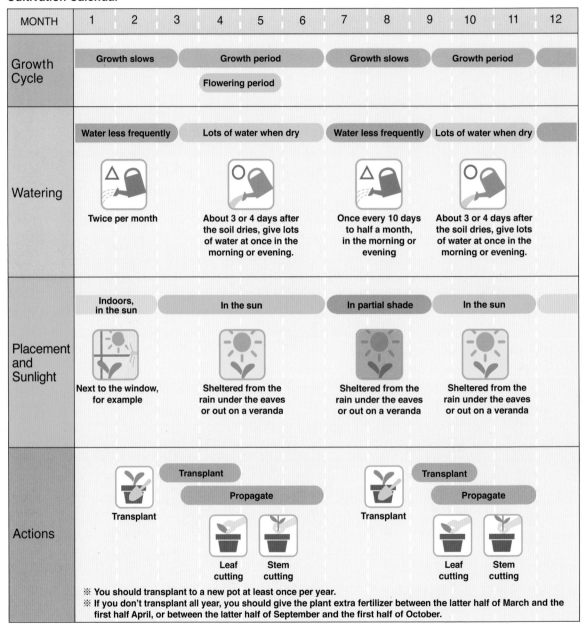

MONTH	1	2	3	4	5	6	7	8	9	10	11	12
Growth Cycle	Growth slows			Growth period			Growth slows			Growth period		
				Flowering period								
Watering	Water less frequently			Lots of water when dry			Water less frequently			Lots of water when dry		
	Twice per month			About 3 or 4 days after the soil dries, give lots of water at once in the morning or evening.			Once every 10 days to half a month, in the morning or evening			About 3 or 4 days after the soil dries, give lots of water at once in the morning or evening.		
Placement and Sunlight	Indoors, in the sun			In the sun			In partial shade			In the sun		
	Next to the window, for example			Sheltered from the rain under the eaves or out on a veranda			Sheltered from the rain under the eaves or out on a veranda			Sheltered from the rain under the eaves or out on a veranda		
Actions			Transplant						Transplant			
				Propagate						Propagate		
		Transplant		Leaf cutting / Stem cutting				Transplant		Leaf cutting / Stem cutting		

※ You should transplant to a new pot at least once per year.
※ If you don't transplant all year, you should give the plant extra fertilizer between the latter half of March and the first half April, or between the latter half of September and the first half of October.

Succulent Advice Q&A **Q** The stem has grown too long and become weak!

 A The stem of this variety grows easily, so you should cut the stem in the middle and replant the top part. Cut off the upper part of the stem with the leaves, let the cut end dry for about a week, and then insert the stem into damp soil. If you continue to grow the remaining lower segment of the stem, it will soon produce axillary buds, and you can propagate it.

Crossbreeding different genera is quite popular. From now on, you can look forward to the appearance of beautiful new hybrids as well.

Members of the *Graptopetalum* Genus

G. mendozae

G. "Debbie"

G. "Peach Hime"

G. pentandrum

G. amethystinum

G. "Bronze Hime"

Pachyphytum oviferum "Hoshibijin"

Characteristics of Hoshibijin

Pachyphytum means "thick plant," and as the name implies, these plants feature round, thick leaves. Hoshibijin is a representative variety for the genus, and its delightful shape is a big hit. The surface of the leaves is beautiful, as if it had been lightly brushed with moon dust; however, the powder comes off to the touch, which leaves unsightly spots, so handle the plant carefully.

Level of Difficulty	Flowering	Native Region
★	Spring	
Easy	Apr.–May	Mexico

Points to Check when Buying

Avoid buying stretched plants where there is a lot of space between the leaves and where the leaves are a pale yellow-green color.

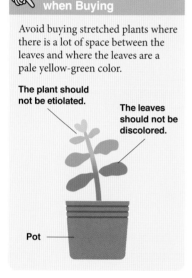

The plant should not be etiolated.

The leaves should not be discolored.

Pot

Soil Composition

Mix 5 parts small-grain Akadama, 3 parts Kanuma soil, and 2 parts mulch for a ratio that has good drainage, water retention, and breathability. Add a layer of gravel like large-grain Akadama or pumice to the bottom of the pot.

Sprinkle in an appropriate amount of granular fertilizer. You can also use liquid fertilizer.

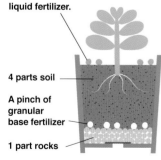

4 parts soil

A pinch of granular base fertilizer

1 part rocks

Fertilizer

When you transplant a succulent, add a layer of granular base fertilizer on top of the layer of gravel.

How to Transplant

The stem grows easily and tends to fall over, so take a stem cutting for transplanting. Remove any darkened and rotten roots, massage out the old soil, and transfer the plant to fresh soil.

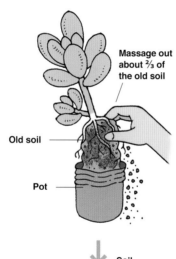

Massage out about ⅔ of the old soil

Old soil

Pot

Soil scoop

Spread the roots apart

Pour in the slightly dampened new soil. When you have finished transplanting, lightly tap the pot to level the soil and place the plant in partial shade to take root.

How to Propagate

Propagation with leaf cuttings or stem cuttings is simple. To use a leaf cutting, remove a plump leaf from the stem and lay it on top of soil for a new plant to take root and sprout. To use a stem cutting, cut off a branch on the side of the stem and insert it in soil.

Leaf Cutting

Place the leaf you removed from the succulent stem on the surface of dampened soil, and after about 10 days the leaf will begin to take root and sprout. When your new plant has grown 4 or 5 leaves, pull it from the soil, taking care not to injure the roots, and transplant it.

Stem Cutting

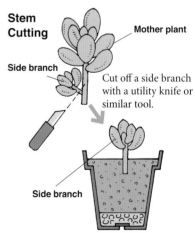

Mother plant

Side branch

Cut off a side branch with a utility knife or similar tool.

Side branch

Let the cut end of the branch dry out for 4–5 days, and then insert the branch into soil. During the first half month until the plant takes root, keep the soil constantly damp and leave the plant in partial shade. After the plant has taken root, you can care for it as usual.

Key Points for Growing Hoshibijin

This variety is very robust and can be easily propagated. Because the stem grows long so easily, expose the plant to lots of sunlight outside during its growing season and keep its shape compact. If you neglect to transplant, the plant will become root bound as the roots run out of space and grow in circles within the pot. This hurts drainage and air circulation in the soil, and can lead to root rot. Be careful of the soil becoming soggy in midsummer, and take your plant inside on cold winter days to prevent freezing.

Cultivation Calendar

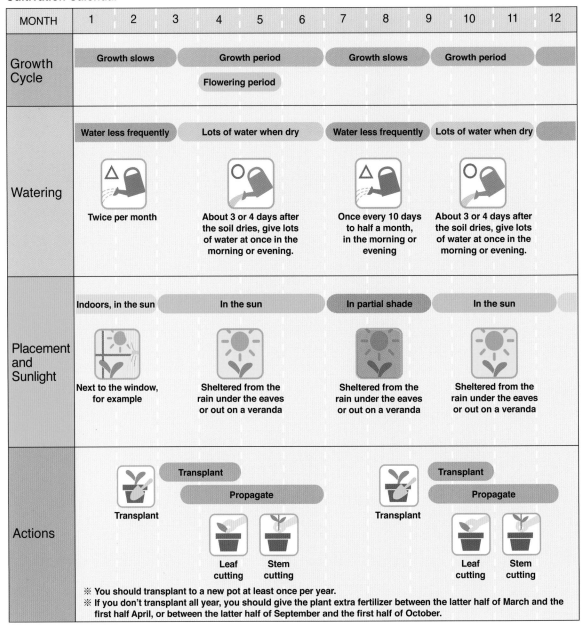

MONTH	1	2	3	4	5	6	7	8	9	10	11	12

Growth Cycle: Growth slows / Growth period / Flowering period / Growth slows / Growth period

Watering:
- Water less frequently — Twice per month
- Lots of water when dry — About 3 or 4 days after the soil dries, give lots of water at once in the morning or evening.
- Water less frequently — Once every 10 days to half a month, in the morning or evening
- Lots of water when dry — About 3 or 4 days after the soil dries, give lots of water at once in the morning or evening.

Placement and Sunlight:
- Indoors, in the sun — Next to the window, for example
- In the sun — Sheltered from the rain under the eaves or out on a veranda
- In partial shade — Sheltered from the rain under the eaves or out on a veranda
- In the sun — Sheltered from the rain under the eaves or out on a veranda

Actions:
- Transplant
- Transplant / Propagate — Leaf cutting / Stem cutting
- Transplant
- Transplant / Propagate — Leaf cutting / Stem cutting

※ You should transplant to a new pot at least once per year.
※ If you don't transplant all year, you should give the plant extra fertilizer between the latter half of March and the first half April, or between the latter half of September and the first half of October.

Succulent Advice Q&A

Q The leaves have lost their powder coating. Will it come back?

A The gentle pastel colors of the leaves are part of the charm of this succulent. When the leaves are touched or are exposed to heavy or long-lasting rain, the powder will come off and expose the bare surface of the leaves. When that happens, the powder will not grow back. You will just have to wait for the blotched leaves to fall and be replaced with new ones as the plant grows.

A flowering Hoshibijin

Gentle shape, gentle colors. Its Japanese
name, "Hoshibijin" or "Star Beauty," likens
this succulent to a beautiful woman.

Members of the *Pachyphytum* genus

P. variegata "Azuma Bijin"

P. "Shireiden"

P. "Momo Bijin"

19

Cotyledon tomentosa "Bear's Paw"

Characteristics of Bear's Paw

The *Cotyledon* genus is a group with an abundance of variations, including plants coated in powder and plants covered in fine hairs. The Bear's Paw is particularly popular among the *Cotyledon* succulents because of its cute leaves, which are shaped like the paws of a bear cub. The image on the left is a variegated type of Bear's Paw that has white patches on the leaves from a mutation.

Level of Difficulty	Flowering	Native Region
★★	Fall	
Standard	Oct.–Nov.	South Africa

Points to Check when Buying

Avoid buying seedlings where the leaves are spread apart on a long, spindly stem, and seedlings where the bottom leaves have fallen off and the stem is sticking out bare.

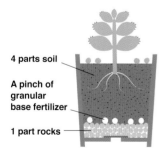

The plant should not be etiolated.

The leaves should not be discolored.

Pot

Soil Composition

Mix 5 parts small-grain Akadama, 3 parts Kanuma soil, and 2 parts mulch for a ratio that has good drainage, water retention, and breathability. Add a layer of gravel like large-grain Akadama or pumice to the bottom of the pot.

4 parts soil

A pinch of granular base fertilizer

1 part rocks

Fertilizer

When you transplant a succulent, add a layer of granular base fertilizer on top of the layer of gravel.

How to Transplant

The best time for transplanting is spring or fall. Pull out the plant, remove any darkened roots, massage out the old soil, and then place the plant in fresh soil. Start watering after about one week.

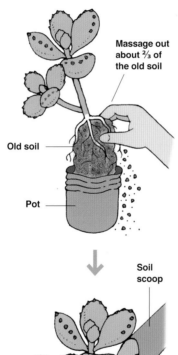

Massage out about ⅔ of the old soil

Old soil

Pot

Soil scoop

Spread the roots apart

Pour in the slightly dampened new soil. When you have finished transplanting, lightly tap the pot to level the soil and place the plant in partial shade to take root.

How to Propagate

You can propagate these succulents from leaf cuttings or stem cuttings. To use a leaf cutting, remove a leaf from the plant, lay it on soil, and place it in partial shade. To use a stem cutting, cut off a side branch with leaves attached, let the cut end dry, and insert it into dampened soil.

Leaf Cutting

Place the leaf you removed from the succulent stem on the surface of dampened soil, and after about 10 days the leaf will begin to take root and sprout. When your new plant has grown 4 or 5 leaves, pull it from the soil, taking care not to injure the roots, and transplant it.

Stem Cutting

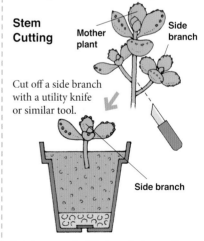

Mother plant

Side branch

Cut off a side branch with a utility knife or similar tool.

Side branch

Let the cut end of the branch dry out for 4–5 days, and then insert the branch into soil. During the first half month until the plant takes root, keep the soil constantly damp and leave the plant in partial shade. After the plant has taken root, you can care for it as usual.

Key Points for Growing Bear's Paw

Grow your succulent in a sunny place during its growing seasons of spring and fall. When the top soil gets dry, wait 3–4 days and then give the plant lots of water. Bear's Paw enters a near dormant state in summer, so if it is exposed to harsh sunlight its leaves will become sunburned and fall off. Move the plant to partial shade and cut back on watering for the rest of the summer. The succulent's growth will slow down in winter, so water it less frequently than in fall. Take the plant inside at night to prevent freezing.

Cultivation Calendar

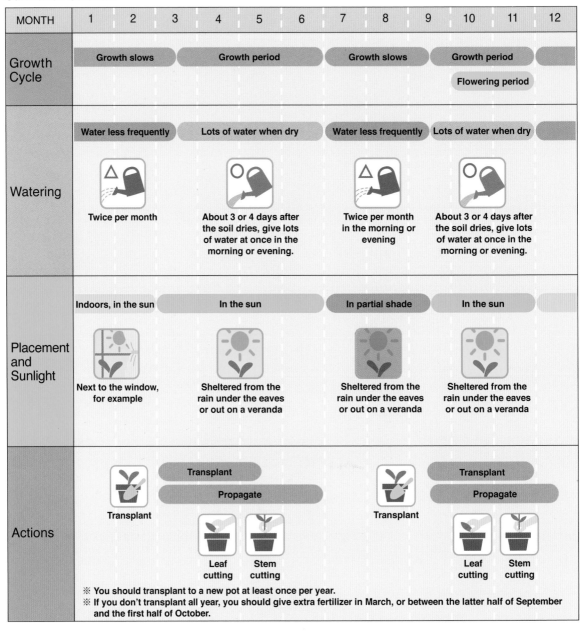

MONTH	1	2	3	4	5	6	7	8	9	10	11	12
Growth Cycle	Growth slows		Growth period			Growth slows			Growth period		Flowering period	
Watering	Water less frequently — Twice per month		Lots of water when dry — About 3 or 4 days after the soil dries, give lots of water at once in the morning or evening.			Water less frequently — Twice per month in the morning or evening			Lots of water when dry — About 3 or 4 days after the soil dries, give lots of water at once in the morning or evening.			
Placement and Sunlight	Indoors, in the sun — Next to the window, for example		In the sun — Sheltered from the rain under the eaves or out on a veranda			In partial shade — Sheltered from the rain under the eaves or out on a veranda			In the sun — Sheltered from the rain under the eaves or out on a veranda			
Actions	Transplant		Transplant / Propagate — Leaf cutting, Stem cutting				Transplant		Transplant / Propagate — Leaf cutting, Stem cutting			

※ You should transplant to a new pot at least once per year.
※ If you don't transplant all year, you should give extra fertilizer in March, or between the latter half of September and the first half of October.

Succulent Advice Q&A

Q I was growing my plant in a pot without any holes in the bottom, and the leaves fell off!

A Even if you tip the pot over and drain out the excess water every time you water the plant, if there isn't good breathability and drainage in the pot, there is a possibility that the inside soil is staying soggy and that the plant has developed root rot. Try to prevent the soil from staying warm and moist by watering less frequently or by transplanting your succulent to a soil with good drainage and breathability in a pot with a hole in the bottom.

The leaves of this plant look like the paws of an adorable bear cub.

Members of the *Cotyledon* Genus

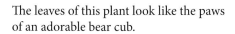

C. orbiculata

C. papillaris

C. undulata

C. pendens

C. undulata variegata

C. tomentosa "Bear's Paw" (without the white patches)

23

Kalanchoe tomentosa "Panda Plant"

Characteristics of Panda Plant

Common *Kalanchoe* varieties (hybrids) were bred selectively as flowering succulents and can now be found all over in a variety of colors. Panda Plant is a charming variety from this genus that got its name from the characteristic white hairs that cover its leaves. This is only one variety among a myriad of diverse types of *Kalanchoe*. Panda Plant originated in the warmth of Madagascar and is sensitive to cold, so take care not to let your succulent freeze.

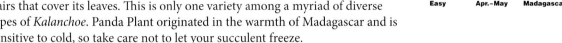

Level of Difficulty	Flowering	Native Region
★ Easy	Spring Apr.–May	Madagascar

Points to Check when Buying

The leaves should be thick and full. Avoid buying seedlings where the stem is stretched and there is a lot of space between the leaves.

The plant should not be etiolated.

The leaves should not be discolored.

Pot

Soil Composition

Mix 5 parts small-grain Akadama, 3 parts Kanuma soil, and 2 parts mulch for a ratio that has good drainage, water retention, and breathability. Add a layer of gravel like large-grain Akadama or pumice to the bottom of the pot.

Sprinkle in an appropriate amount of granular fertilizer. You can also use liquid fertilizer.

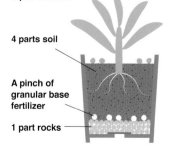

4 parts soil

A pinch of granular base fertilizer

1 part rocks

Fertilizer

When you transplant a succulent, add a layer of granular base fertilizer on top of the layer of gravel.

How to Transplant

Pull the plant out of its pot and check the condition of the roots, removing any darkened ones. Carefully massage out the old soil, spread the roots apart in the new pot, and pour in fresh soil.

Massage out about ⅔ of the old soil

Old soil

Pot

Soil scoop

Spread the roots apart

Pour in the slightly dampened new soil. When you have finished transplanting, lightly tap the pot to level the soil and place the plant in partial shade to take root.

How to Propagate

The best time to propagate is in the spring or fall. To use a leaf cutting, place a leaf taken from the lower part of the plant on top of dampened soil. To use a stem cutting, cut off a side branch that has leaves attached and let it dry for a few days before placing it in dampened soil. Let it take root and sprout in partial shade.

Leaf Cutting

Place the leaf you removed from the succulent stem on the surface of dampened soil, and after about 10 days the leaf will begin to take root and sprout. When your new plant has grown 4 or 5 leaves, pull it from the soil, taking care not to injure the roots, and transplant it.

Stem Cutting

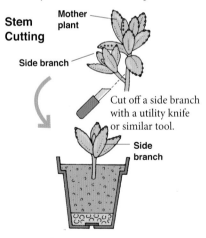

Mother plant

Side branch

Cut off a side branch with a utility knife or similar tool.

Side branch

Let the cut end of the branch dry out for 4–5 days, and then insert the branch into soil. During the first half month until the plant takes root, keep the soil constantly damp and leave the plant in partial shade. After the plant has taken root, you can care for it as usual.

25

Key Points for Growing Panda Plant

This is a robust plant, so during its growing period you can place it in an sunny, well-ventilated area and expose it to direct sunlight. Give the plant lots of water at once about 3–4 days after the top soil dries out. However, be careful not to give too much water, or fungus can form and cause root rot. Particularly during midsummer when the succulent's growth slows, you should keep the plant in partial shade and make sure not to water it during the day. Panda Plant is also sensitive to cold, so take it inside at night.

Cultivation Calendar

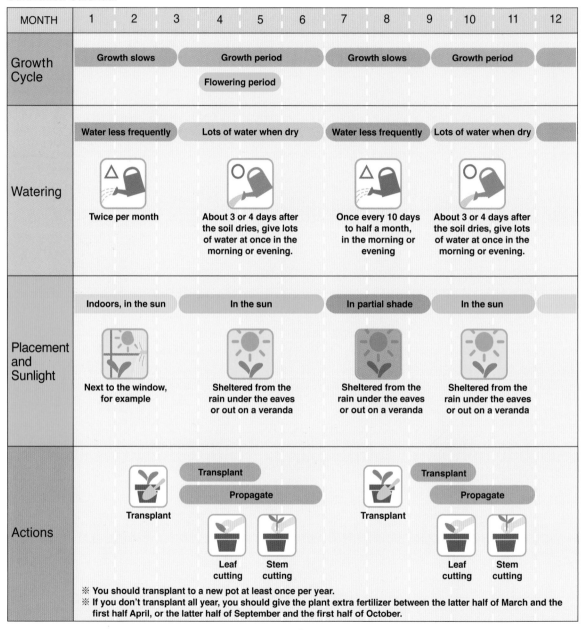

MONTH	1	2	3	4	5	6	7	8	9	10	11	12
Growth Cycle	Growth slows		Growth period				Growth slows		Growth period			
			Flowering period									
Watering	Water less frequently		Lots of water when dry				Water less frequently		Lots of water when dry			
	Twice per month		About 3 or 4 days after the soil dries, give lots of water at once in the morning or evening.				Once every 10 days to half a month, in the morning or evening		About 3 or 4 days after the soil dries, give lots of water at once in the morning or evening.			
Placement and Sunlight	Indoors, in the sun		In the sun				In partial shade		In the sun			
	Next to the window, for example		Sheltered from the rain under the eaves or out on a veranda				Sheltered from the rain under the eaves or out on a veranda		Sheltered from the rain under the eaves or out on a veranda			
Actions	Transplant		Transplant				Transplant		Transplant			
			Propagate						Propagate			
			Leaf cutting / Stem cutting						Leaf cutting / Stem cutting			

※ You should transplant to a new pot at least once per year.
※ If you don't transplant all year, you should give the plant extra fertilizer between the latter half of March and the first half April, or the latter half of September and the first half of October.

Succulent Advice Q&A **Q** I left my succulent outside during winter and it froze!

A These plants come from a tropical climate and are sensitive to cold, so once they freeze they are practically impossible to save. You should bring your Panda Plant inside during winter nights. If you water less frequently during the winter, there will be less water inside the plant, mitigating the harm caused by the plant freezing. However, a plant kept inside during the winter might suffer from insufficient sunlight, so be careful that the leaves don't sunburn once spring arrives.

The velvety feel of the leaves is like
an adorable panda's fur.

Members of the *Kalanchoe* Genus

K. tomentosa "Giant Rabbit"

K. eriophylla

K. daigremontiana

K. thyrsiflora variegata

K. humilis

Common *Kalanchoe* (hybrid)

27

Senecio rowleyanus **"String of Pearls"**

Characteristics of String of Pearls

String of Pearls is a member of the *Asteraceae* family. Its tubular flowers bloom from fall to winter, and have an unusual shape and way of attaching to the plant. The round leaves and dainty vines stretch in all directions and dangle over the side of the pot, so you can take in the beauty of the String of Pearls as a hanging plant. There are a variety of plants in this genus, so it can be quite interesting to try collecting different varieties. You can find such plants in dry regions of places like Africa, Madagascar, and Mexico.

Level of Difficulty	Flowering	Native Region
★	Winter	
Easy	Jan.–Mar.	Namibia

Points to Check when Buying

Avoid buying during the summer, when the plant is weak. A seedling that looks lifeless and has few leaves is weakened and suffering from root rot.

The leaves should not be discolored.

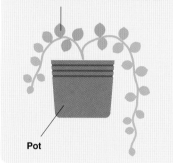

Pot

Soil Composition

Mix 5 parts small-grain Akadama, 3 parts Kanuma soil, and 2 parts mulch for a ratio that has good drainage, water retention, and breathability. Add a layer of gravel like large-grain Akadama or pumice to the bottom of the pot.

Sprinkle in an appropriate amount of granular fertilizer. You can also use liquid fertilizer.

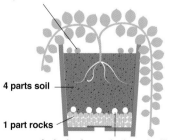

4 parts soil

1 part rocks

A pinch of granular base fertilizer

Fertilizer

When you transplant a succulent, add a layer of granular base fertilizer on top of the layer of gravel.

How to Transplant

The best time for transplanting is spring or fall. Pull out the plant, then carefully break up and throw away about ⅔ of the old soil in the roots. Pour fresh soil into the pot, and when the plant gets larger, move it to a larger pot.

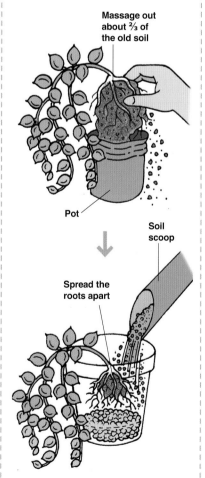

Massage out about ⅔ of the old soil

Pot

Soil scoop

Spread the roots apart

Pour in the slightly dampened new soil. When you have finished transplanting, lightly tap the pot to level the soil and place the plant in partial shade to take root.

How to Propagate

In addition to propagating from a leaf cutting, you can also take one of the long vines and insert its stem into fresh soil as a stem cutting. For large plants, you can also propagate through division.

Leaf Cutting

Place the leaf you removed from the succulent stem on the surface of dampened soil, and after about 10 days the leaf will begin to take root and sprout. When your new plant has grown 4 or 5 leaves, pull it from the soil, taking care not to injure the roots, and transplant it.

Stem Cutting

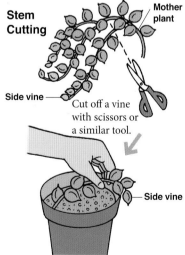

Mother plant

Side vine

Cut off a vine with scissors or a similar tool.

Side vine

If you let the cut vine creep across the surface of the dampened soil, it will take root after about 10 days, so just leave the plant to grow.
※ When the plant has produced roots, begin watering it normally.

Key Points for Growing String of Pearls

String of Pearls is robust and easy to grow, so in the spring or fall you can even admire your plant hanging from a tree or elsewhere outside. Your plant will survive being exposed to rain. String of Pearls plants are weak to hot and humid conditions and will wilt, so if you live in an area with such summers, move your plant to a well-ventilated area in partial shade and be conservative when watering. Keep the soil from staying hot and moist to prevent fungus from growing and causing root rot. String of Pearls is relatively strong against the cold, so if you just water the plant less frequently in winter it can even withstand the damage caused by frost.

Cultivation Calendar

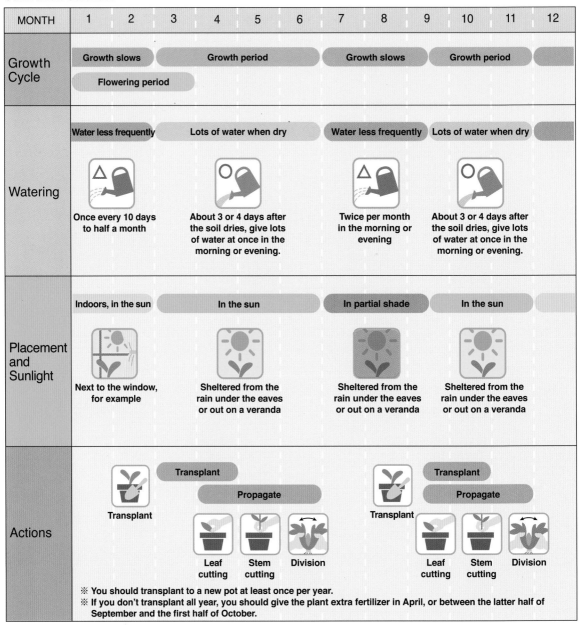

MONTH	1	2	3	4	5	6	7	8	9	10	11	12

Growth Cycle
- Growth slows (1–2) | Growth period (3–6) | Growth slows (7–8) | Growth period (9–11)
- Flowering period (2–3)

Watering
- Water less frequently (1–3): Once every 10 days to half a month
- Lots of water when dry (4–6): About 3 or 4 days after the soil dries, give lots of water at once in the morning or evening.
- Water less frequently (7–8): Twice per month in the morning or evening
- Lots of water when dry (9–11): About 3 or 4 days after the soil dries, give lots of water at once in the morning or evening.

Placement and Sunlight
- Indoors, in the sun (1–3): Next to the window, for example
- In the sun (4–6): Sheltered from the rain under the eaves or out on a veranda
- In partial shade (7–8): Sheltered from the rain under the eaves or out on a veranda
- In the sun (9–11): Sheltered from the rain under the eaves or out on a veranda

Actions
- Transplant
- Transplant, Propagate (Leaf cutting, Stem cutting, Division)
- Transplant
- Transplant, Propagate (Leaf cutting, Stem cutting, Division)

※ You should transplant to a new pot at least once per year.
※ If you don't transplant all year, you should give the plant extra fertilizer in April, or between the latter half of September and the first half of October.

Succulent Advice Q&A

Q I set my succulent out in the midsummer sun and its leaves turned brown!

A String of Pearls comes from a dry climate and is sensitive to hot and humid summers, so if you placed a weakened plant in harsh sunlight it was probably sunburned. This is all the more likely because the roots are weakened at this time as well. Move the plant to a cool, breezy area in partial shade, cut back on the watering, and protect against root rot caused by soggy soil for the rest of the summer.

Another name for this plant is "String of Beads." Its flowers shaped like a painter's brush are captivating as well.

Flowering String of Pearls

Members of the *Senecio* Genus

S. haworthii

S. keiniiformis

S. articulatus

31

Othonna capensis "Ruby Necklace"

Characteristics of Ruby Necklace

Ruby Necklace is a member of the *Asteraceae* family, and even in the middle of winter this plant will produce small, yellow, chrysanthemum-like flowers one after another. Its stems are purple vines that creep out and spread in all directions. You can let the vines dangle from the pot and enjoy Ruby Necklace as a hanging plant. There is also an *O. capensis* that has the same shape as Ruby Necklace but is completely green in color. Both are robust plants and are strong against the cold.

Level of Difficulty	Flowering	Native Region
★	Winter	
Easy	Dec.–Mar.	Africa

Points to Check when Buying

Avoid plants where the stem has grown too long and spindly. Instead, select ones that are full of life and have lots of leaves.

The leaves should not be discolored.

Pot

Soil Composition

Mix 5 parts small-grain Akadama, 3 parts Kanuma soil, and 2 parts mulch for a ratio that has good drainage, water retention, and breathability. Add a layer of gravel like large-grain Akadama or pumice to the bottom of the pot.

Sprinkle in an appropriate amount of granular fertilizer. You can also use liquid fertilizer.

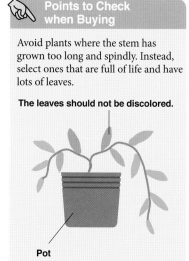

4 parts soil

1 part rocks

A pinch of granular base fertilizer

Fertilizer

When you transplant a succulent, add a layer of granular base fertilizer on top of the layer of gravel.

How to Transplant

When the roots have stretched out in their container, pull out the plant and massage the old soil from the roots. Spread the roots apart and add in new soil. Leave the plant in partial shade for about a week, then move it to a sunny area and begin watering.

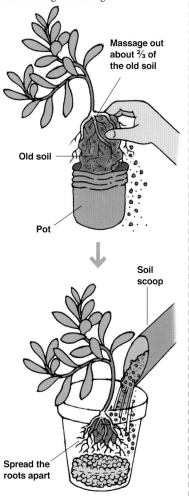

Massage out about ⅔ of the old soil

Old soil

Pot

Soil scoop

Spread the roots apart

Pour in the slightly dampened new soil. When you have finished transplanting, lightly tap the pot to level the soil and place the plant in partial shade to take root.

How to Propagate

You can remove a single leaf from a stem or cut one of the vines in the middle to use as a cutting. For plants that have grown large, you can also propagate through division.

Leaf Cutting

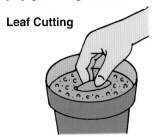

Place the leaf you removed from the succulent stem on the surface of dampened soil, and after about 10 days the leaf will begin to take root and sprout. When your new plant has grown 4 or 5 leaves, pull it from the soil, taking care not to injure the roots, and transplant it.

Stem Cutting

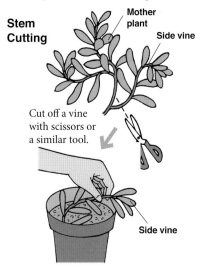

Mother plant

Side vine

Cut off a vine with scissors or a similar tool.

Side vine

If you let the cut vine creep across the surface of the dampened soil, it will take root after about 10 days, so just leave the plant to grow.

※ When the plant has produced roots, begin watering it normally.

Key Points for Growing Ruby Necklace

This robust plant grows at a rapid pace, so when it fills up its pot, transplant it to a larger one. Ruby Necklace thrives in places with sunlight and good ventilation, so let it sit outside during spring and fall. It should be fine even if exposed to the rain. Growth will slow somewhat during the hot and humid days of midsummer, so move your succulent into partial shade. Fungus can develop and cause root rot if you overwater, so make sure the soil in the pot is completely dry before giving lots of water.

Cultivation Calendar

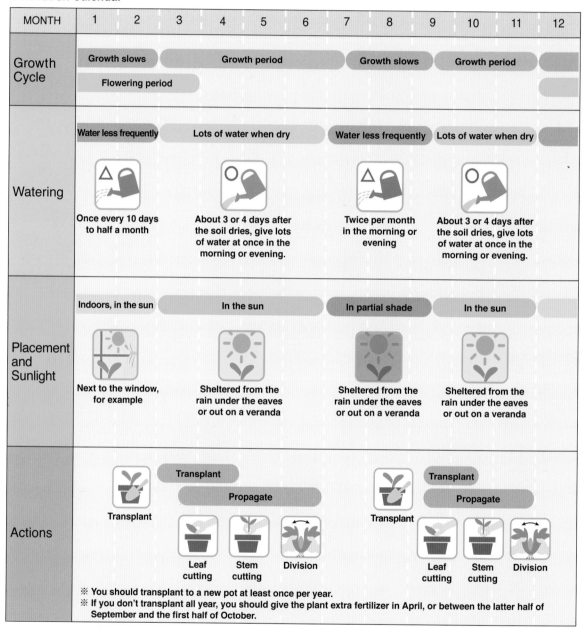

MONTH	1	2	3	4	5	6	7	8	9	10	11	12

Growth Cycle
- Growth slows | Growth period | Growth slows | Growth period
- Flowering period

Watering
- Water less frequently | Lots of water when dry | Water less frequently | Lots of water when dry
- Once every 10 days to half a month
- About 3 or 4 days after the soil dries, give lots of water at once in the morning or evening.
- Twice per month in the morning or evening
- About 3 or 4 days after the soil dries, give lots of water at once in the morning or evening.

Placement and Sunlight
- Indoors, in the sun | In the sun | In partial shade | In the sun
- Next to the window, for example
- Sheltered from the rain under the eaves or out on a veranda
- Sheltered from the rain under the eaves or out on a veranda
- Sheltered from the rain under the eaves or out on a veranda

Actions
- Transplant | Transplant
- Propagate | Propagate
- Transplant | Transplant
- Leaf cutting | Stem cutting | Division | Leaf cutting | Stem cutting | Division

※ You should transplant to a new pot at least once per year.
※ If you don't transplant all year, you should give the plant extra fertilizer in April, or between the latter half of September and the first half of October.

Succulent Advice Q&A

Q My plant's leaves used to be full and plump, but now they've wilted!

A The reason your plant is weakened and wilting may be because it has root rot from overwatering. First, pull the plant from its pot and remove any dark, damaged roots. Then, transplant it to fresh soil. If you transplant during a growth period in spring or fall, resume watering after one week. If you transplant in summer or winter, wait until the plant enters a growth period to resume watering.

34

Ruby Necklace gets its name from the vibrant red of its stems.

Members of the *Othonna* Genus

O. capensis "Little Pickles"

O. clavifolia *Dormant during summer

O. herrei *Dormant during summer

Crassula capitella "**Campfire**"

Characteristics of Campfire

The leaves of this species change color in the cold, dyed a beautiful scarlet as if consumed by flames. It is during this time that the plant is truly worthy of the name "Campfire." Otherwise, the leaves are bright green. These easy-to-grow succulents undergo rapid growth during the growing seasons of spring and fall, and beginning around the end of summer, their stems will stretch up tall and produce little white flowers. These plants originated in South Africa and grow to about 6 inches (15 cm) tall.

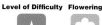

Level of Difficulty	Flowering	Native Region
★	Fall	
Easy	Oct.–Nov.	South Africa

Points to Check when Buying

Avoid buying etiolated seedlings that are too tall and have too much space between the leaves, or that are a pale, yellow-green color around the leaves.

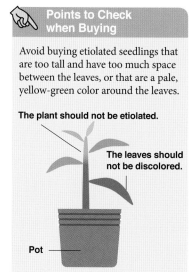

The plant should not be etiolated.

The leaves should not be discolored.

Pot

Soil Composition

Mix 5 parts small-grain Akadama, 3 parts Kanuma soil, and 2 parts mulch for a ratio that has good drainage, water retention, and breathability. Add a layer of gravel like large-grain Akadama or pumice to the bottom of the pot.

Sprinkle in an appropriate amount of granular fertilizer. You can also use liquid fertilizer.

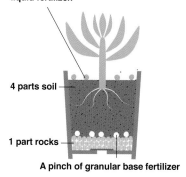

4 parts soil

1 part rocks

A pinch of granular base fertilizer

Fertilizer

When you transplant a succulent, add a layer of granular base fertilizer on top of the layer of gravel.

How to Transplant

Move the succulent from its container to soil. When you pull out the plant, check its roots and remove any darkened or damaged ones before transplanting to the new soil.

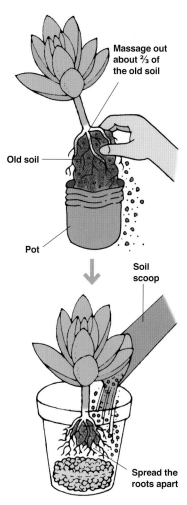

Massage out about ⅔ of the old soil

Old soil

Pot

Soil scoop

Spread the roots apart

Pour in the slightly dampened new soil. When you have finished transplanting, lightly tap the pot to level the soil and place the plant in partial shade to take root.

How to Propagate

You can propagate from a leaf cutting, or cut off a side branch with leaves attached, let the cut end dry for a few days, and insert it into soil. Slightly dampened soil will encourage the plant to take root.

Leaf Cutting

Place the leaf you removed from the succulent stem on the surface of dampened soil, and after about 10 days the leaf will begin to take root and sprout. When your new plant has grown 4 or 5 leaves, pull it from the soil, taking care not to injure the roots, and transplant it.

Stem Cutting

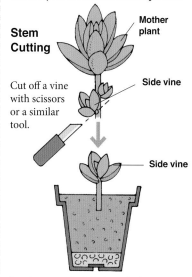

Mother plant

Cut off a vine with scissors or a similar tool.

Side vine

Side vine

Let the cut end of the branch dry out for 4–5 days, and then insert the branch into soil. During the first half month until the plant takes root, keep the soil constantly damp and leave the plant in partial shade. After the plant has taken root, you can care for it as usual.

Key Points for Growing Campfire

Campfire is robust and easy to grow, like Jade Plant, another member of the *Crassula* genus. It can also tolerate rain. Its growth seasons are spring and fall, and you should grow a Campfire succulent in a sunny location. Give your plant lots of water when the top soil dries out. Your plant will manage to survive midsummer one way or another. When fall arrives, it will resume its rapid growth, but when the weather turns cold its growth will slow again and you will need to water it less frequently. Take your succulent inside on nights when the temperature drops below freezing.

Cultivation Calendar

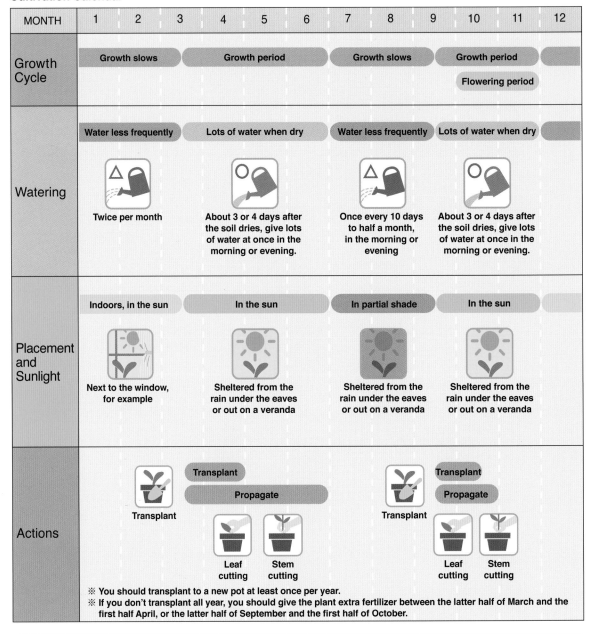

MONTH	1	2	3	4	5	6	7	8	9	10	11	12
Growth Cycle	Growth slows			Growth period			Growth slows			Growth period		
										Flowering period		
Watering	Water less frequently			Lots of water when dry			Water less frequently			Lots of water when dry		
	Twice per month			About 3 or 4 days after the soil dries, give lots of water at once in the morning or evening.			Once every 10 days to half a month, in the morning or evening			About 3 or 4 days after the soil dries, give lots of water at once in the morning or evening.		
Placement and Sunlight	Indoors, in the sun			In the sun			In partial shade			In the sun		
	Next to the window, for example			Sheltered from the rain under the eaves or out on a veranda			Sheltered from the rain under the eaves or out on a veranda			Sheltered from the rain under the eaves or out on a veranda		
Actions	Transplant	Transplant						Transplant	Transplant			
		Propagate		Leaf cutting / Stem cutting					Propagate	Leaf cutting / Stem cutting		

※ You should transplant to a new pot at least once per year.
※ If you don't transplant all year, you should give the plant extra fertilizer between the latter half of March and the first half April, or the latter half of September and the first half of October.

Q Why won't my succulent's leaves turn red, even in the cold?

A Normally, a succulent will take in a lot of sunlight during the fall, and then turn red when a cold spell comes along. However, if you have been growing the plant in the shade or indoors, it may not turn red because of a lack of sunlight. If the plant is etiolated, it is suffering from a lack of sunlight. Also, the leaves will change from red back to their green color in spring, but this is just proof that the plant is active in its growing period and is not a problem.

As the weather grows colder, Campfire becomes a fiery red.

Members of the *Crassula* Genus

C. cordata

C. sarmentosa

C. alba

C. fusca

C. ovata "Variegated Jade Plant"

C. "Morgan's Beauty"

Sedum rubrotinctum "Jelly Bean Plant" /
Variegated *Sedum rubrotinctum* "Aurora" /
Sedum oryzifolium "Tiny Form"

Characteristics of Jelly Bean Plant, Aurora, and Tiny Form

Plants of the *Sedum* genus are also referred to as stonecrops. They are small, creeping succulents that undergo rapid growth during the spring and fall. There are more than 500 varieties of *Sedum* scattered around the world, and Tiny Form can even be found growing wild in Japan. Additionally, Jelly Bean Plant and *Aurora* will turn red as the temperature grows colder. All three produce small, lovely flowers from spring to early summer.

Level of Difficulty	Flowering	Native Region
 ★	Spring	
Easy	Apr.–Jun.	South Africa

Points to Check when Buying

Choose seedlings that have a short stem and are dense with small, round leaves.

The plant should not be etiolated.

The leaves should not be discolored.

Pot

Soil Composition

Mix 5 parts small-grain Akadama, 3 parts Kanuma soil, and 2 parts mulch for a ratio that has good drainage, water retention, and breathability. Add a layer of gravel like large-grain Akadama or pumice to the bottom of the pot.

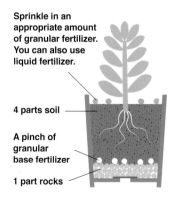

Sprinkle in an appropriate amount of granular fertilizer. You can also use liquid fertilizer.

4 parts soil

A pinch of granular base fertilizer

1 part rocks

Fertilizer

When you transplant a succulent, add a layer of granular base fertilizer on top of the layer of gravel.

How to Transplant

If the plant becomes root bound, pull it out and massage the soil from the roots. Spread the roots apart and pour in fresh soil. Leave your succulent in partial shade for 3–4 days before you start watering it.

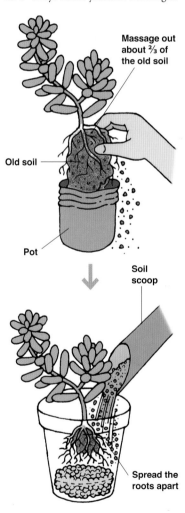

Massage out about ⅔ of the old soil

Old soil

Pot

Soil scoop

Spread the roots apart

Pour in the slightly dampened new soil. When you have finished transplanting, lightly tap the pot to level the soil and place the plant in partial shade to take root.

How to Propagate

These succulents are simple to propagate. To propagate from a leaf cutting, just pluck off a leaf and lay it in soil for it to grow roots and sprout. To propagate from a stem cutting, cut off a long stem and insert it into soil to take root.

Leaf Cutting

Place the leaf you removed from the succulent stem on the surface of dampened soil, and after about 10 days the leaf will begin to take root and sprout. When your new plant has grown 4 or 5 leaves, pull it from the soil, taking care not to injure the roots, and transplant it.

Stem Cutting

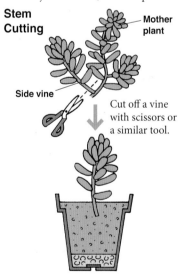

Mother plant

Side vine

Cut off a vine with scissors or a similar tool.

Let the cut end of the branch dry out for 4–5 days, and then insert the branch into soil. During the first half month until the plant takes root, keep the soil constantly damp and leave the plant in partial shade. After the plant has taken root, you can care for it as usual.

Key Points for Growing Jelly Bean Plant, Aurora, and Tiny Form

These species are robust and easy to grow. They grow rapidly during the spring and fall, so plant them in soil with good drainage and breathability. With the exception of hot summer days, you can keep these succulents in a place with lots of sunshine. They are sensitive to heat and humidity, so keep them in a well-ventilated area in partial shade for the summer. They are strong enough against the cold that you can set them out in the sun even in winter, but they will mostly stop growing during that time. Be careful not to overwater during summer and winter.

Cultivation Calendar

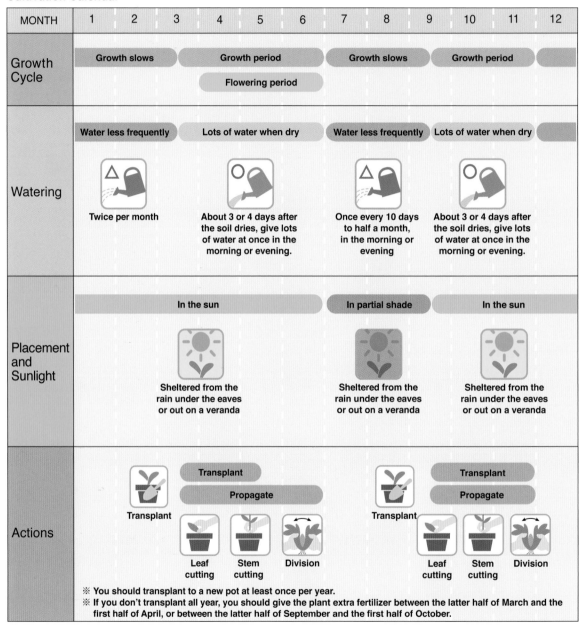

MONTH	1	2	3	4	5	6	7	8	9	10	11	12

Growth Cycle
- Growth slows (months 1–3)
- Growth period (months 4–6)
- Flowering period
- Growth slows (months 7–9)
- Growth period (months 10–12)

Watering
- Water less frequently — Twice per month
- Lots of water when dry — About 3 or 4 days after the soil dries, give lots of water at once in the morning or evening.
- Water less frequently — Once every 10 days to half a month, in the morning or evening
- Lots of water when dry — About 3 or 4 days after the soil dries, give lots of water at once in the morning or evening.

Placement and Sunlight
- In the sun — Sheltered from the rain under the eaves or out on a veranda
- In partial shade — Sheltered from the rain under the eaves or out on a veranda
- In the sun — Sheltered from the rain under the eaves or out on a veranda

Actions
- Transplant / Propagate
- Transplant
- Leaf cutting / Stem cutting / Division
- Transplant / Propagate
- Transplant
- Leaf cutting / Stem cutting / Division

※ You should transplant to a new pot at least once per year.
※ If you don't transplant all year, you should give the plant extra fertilizer between the latter half of March and the first half of April, or between the latter half of September and the first half of October.

Succulent Advice Q&A

Q My plant shrunk during midsummer!

A These plants are sensitive to the heat and high humidity of midsummer, so sometimes they develop root rot from soggy soil. Also, even plants that were full of energy in spring can weaken in the heat and shrink in size. It should be safer to move your plant to a well-ventilated area in partial shade. Jelly Bean Plant and Tiny Form are relatively hardy and can last the summer, but Aurora is somewhat weak, so be careful.

Sedum plants are very resilient to the cold and are easy to grow. I recommend them as introductory succulents for beginners.

Jelly Bean Plant   **Tiny Form**   **Aurora**

Members of the *Sedum* Genus

S. hernandezii

S. corynephyllum

S. "Little Gem"

S. palmeri

S. adolphii

S. dasyphyllum

43

Spring/Fall
Types

Aeonium haworthii "Tricolor"

Characteristics of Tricolor

This variety comes from the Canary Islands off the northwestern coast of the African continent. These arid islands have a warm climate with temperatures around 59F/15C to 77F/25C. The leaves of Tricolor *Aeonium* are not very thick, and the slender stems can grow to a height of 20 inches (50 cm) or more. These plants produce several stems that grow up from their bases. If you expose your succulent to a lot of sunlight, its leaves will change into beautiful colors during the winter.

Level of Difficulty	Flowering	Native Region
Easy	Spring	Canary Islands
	Apr.–May	

Points to Check when Buying

The stems grow easily, so short, energetic seedlings with their leaves unfolded are best. Avoid seedlings where the stems are stretched too tall.

The plant should not be etiolated.

The leaves should not be discolored.

Pot

Soil Composition

Mix 5 parts small-grain Akadama, 3 parts Kanuma soil, and 2 parts mulch for a ratio that has good drainage, water retention, and breathability. Add a layer of gravel like large-grain Akadama or pumice to the bottom of the pot.

Sprinkle in an appropriate amount of granular fertilizer. You can also use liquid fertilizer.

4 parts soil

A pinch of granular base fertilizer

1 part rocks

Fertilizer

When you transplant a succulent, add a layer of granular base fertilizer on top of the layer of gravel.

How to Transplant

If the plant becomes root bound, pull it out from its pot, massage about ⅔ of the old soil from the roots, and transfer it to fresh soil. Begin watering after about 4–5 days.

Massage out about ⅔ of the old soil

Old soil

Pot

Soil scoop

Spread the roots apart

Pour in the slightly dampened new soil. When you have finished transplanting, lightly tap the pot to level the soil and place the plant in partial shade to take root.

How to Propagate

There will be many side stems, so cut off one that has leaves attached, let the cut end dry for several days, and then insert your new cutting into soil. Keep the soil slightly damp to encourage your plant to take root.

Leaf Cutting

Place the leaf you removed from the succulent stem on the surface of dampened soil, and after about 10 days the leaf will begin to take root and sprout. When your new plant has grown 4 or 5 leaves, pull it from the soil, taking care not to injure the roots, and transplant it.

Stem Cutting

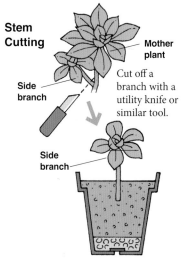

Mother plant

Side branch

Cut off a branch with a utility knife or similar tool.

Side branch

Let the cut end of the branch dry out for 4–5 days, and then insert the branch into soil. During the first half month until the plant takes root, keep the soil constantly damp and leave the plant in partial shade. After the plant has taken root, you can care for it as usual.

Key Points for Growing Tricolor

Expose your plant to lots of sunlight outdoors during spring and fall. This variety does poorly against heat and high humidity and will become weaker as summer approaches, so move your succulent to partial shade and water it less frequently until summer ends. On the other hand, this species is strong against the cold and will keep growing during winter, but bring it inside at night to prevent it from freezing or developing frost. Be careful not to overwater during summer or winter. Among the plants in the *Aeonium* genus, *A. haworthii* "Tricolor" and *A. arboreum* "Zwartkop" are especially robust.

Cultivation Calendar

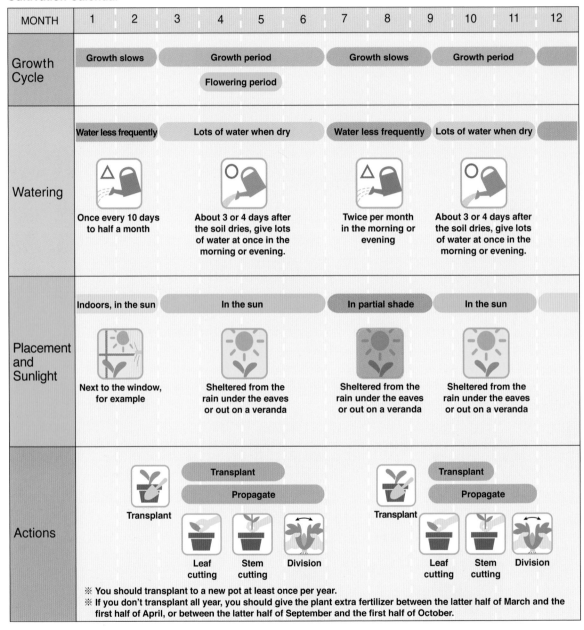

MONTH	1	2	3	4	5	6	7	8	9	10	11	12
Growth Cycle	Growth slows		Growth period				Growth slows		Growth period			
			Flowering period									
Watering	Water less frequently		Lots of water when dry				Water less frequently		Lots of water when dry			
	Once every 10 days to half a month		About 3 or 4 days after the soil dries, give lots of water at once in the morning or evening.				Twice per month in the morning or evening		About 3 or 4 days after the soil dries, give lots of water at once in the morning or evening.			
Placement and Sunlight	Indoors, in the sun		In the sun				In partial shade		In the sun			
	Next to the window, for example		Sheltered from the rain under the eaves or out on a veranda				Sheltered from the rain under the eaves or out on a veranda		Sheltered from the rain under the eaves or out on a veranda			

Actions

Transplant / Propagate — Transplant — Leaf cutting, Stem cutting, Division (two periods: around months 3–6 and around months 9–11)

※ You should transplant to a new pot at least once per year.
※ If you don't transplant all year, you should give the plant extra fertilizer between the latter half of March and the first half of April, or between the latter half of September and the first half of October.

Succulent Advice Q&A

Q My plant lost its leaves and started drooping in summer!

A When summer arrives, the plant is going to grow weaker no matter what, so this is no particular cause for concern. Move the plant to a well-ventilated area in partial shade and water it less frequently. Water during the morning or evening instead of midday in the heat. When fall comes and the temperature cools down, your succulent will revive and return to its usual active state.

Spring/Fall Types

Tricolor after the leaves have changed colors

When a cold wave hits, the leaves are dyed a slight crimson.

Members of the *Aeonium* Genus

A. "Lemonade"

A. tabuliforme ※ Semi-dormant during summer

A. "Sunburst"

A. dodrantale ※ Dormant during summer

A. castello-paivae variegata "Suncup"

A. arboreum "Zwartkop"

47

Plectranthus aromaticus

Characteristics of *P. aromaticus*

As the name implies, the leaves of *P. aromaticus* have a pleasant aroma, and this refined fragrance attracts even those who aren't usually fans of succulents. Perennial plants can either creep along the ground or grow erect, and *P. aromaticus* grows upward. This species is very robust and can grow even if exposed to the rain, but it does poorly in heat and high humidity and will need to be moved to partial shade during such times. It is also slightly sensitive to the cold, so you should bring it inside at night.

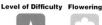

Level of Difficulty	Flowering	Native Region
★ Easy	Spring Apr.–Jun.	South Africa

Points to Check when Buying

The leaves should be luxuriant and the plant full of life. Avoid plants where the stem is stretched long and spindly.

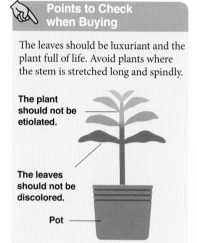

The plant should not be etiolated.

The leaves should not be discolored.

Pot

Soil Composition

Mix 5 parts small-grain Akadama, 3 parts Kanuma soil, and 2 parts mulch for a ratio that has good drainage, water retention, and breathability. Add a layer of gravel like large-grain Akadama or pumice to the bottom of the pot.

Sprinkle in an appropriate amount of granular fertilizer. You can also use liquid fertilizer.

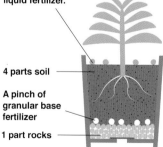

4 parts soil

A pinch of granular base fertilizer

1 part rocks

Fertilizer

When you transplant a succulent, add a layer of granular base fertilizer on top of the layer of gravel.

How to Transplant

If the plant is in a pot, pull it out and massage out about ⅔ of the old soil stuck to the roots. Switch to the new pot, spread the roots apart, and pour in fresh soil.

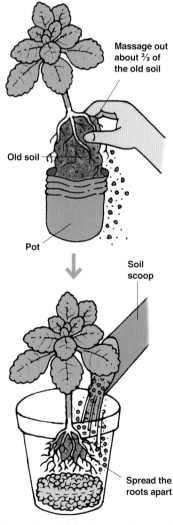

Massage out about ⅔ of the old soil

Old soil

Pot

Soil scoop

Spread the roots apart

Pour in the slightly dampened new soil. When you have finished transplanting, lightly tap the pot to level the soil and place the plant in partial shade to take root.

How to Propagate

There will be many branching stems, so cut off a branch with leaves attached, and then either insert it into soil or let it grow roots in water before planting it in soil.

Leaf Cutting

Place the leaf you removed from the succulent stem on the surface of dampened soil, and after about 10 days the leaf will begin to take root and sprout. When your new plant has grown 4 or 5 leaves, pull it from the soil, taking care not to injure the roots, and transplant it.

Stem Cutting

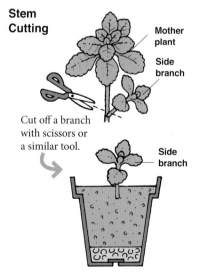

Mother plant

Side branch

Cut off a branch with scissors or a similar tool.

Side branch

Let the cut end of the branch dry out for 2–3 days, and then insert the branch into soil. Keep the soil constantly damp and leave the plant in partial shade to take root. You can also let the plant develop roots in water.

Key Points for Growing *P. aromaticus*

P. aromaticus is a robust species, so during its growth season, it can grow even when exposed to rain. However, if it appears the rain will continue for a long time, move your succulent under the eaves and out of the rain to prevent root rot. These plants enjoy direct sunlight but can be sunburned by the harsh sunlight of midsummer, so move your plant into partial shade and avoid watering during the hottest part of the day. These plants are also slightly sensitive to cold, so move your succulent to a sunny place indoors during the winter and water it less frequently.

Cultivation Calendar

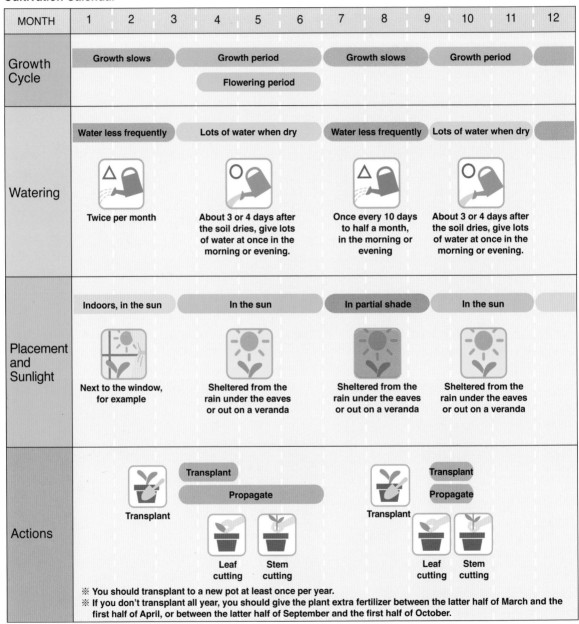

MONTH	1	2	3	4	5	6	7	8	9	10	11	12
Growth Cycle	Growth slows			Growth period			Growth slows			Growth period		
				Flowering period								
Watering	Water less frequently			Lots of water when dry			Water less frequently			Lots of water when dry		
	Twice per month			About 3 or 4 days after the soil dries, give lots of water at once in the morning or evening.			Once every 10 days to half a month, in the morning or evening			About 3 or 4 days after the soil dries, give lots of water at once in the morning or evening.		
Placement and Sunlight	Indoors, in the sun			In the sun			In partial shade			In the sun		
	Next to the window, for example			Sheltered from the rain under the eaves or out on a veranda			Sheltered from the rain under the eaves or out on a veranda			Sheltered from the rain under the eaves or out on a veranda		
Actions	Transplant	Transplant					Transplant	Transplant				
		Propagate						Propagate				
				Leaf cutting	Stem cutting					Leaf cutting	Stem cutting	

※ You should transplant to a new pot at least once per year.
※ If you don't transplant all year, you should give the plant extra fertilizer between the latter half of March and the first half of April, or between the latter half of September and the first half of October.

Succulent Advice Q&A **(Q)** My plant's stems grew too long, and now they stand out too much and are hard to look at!

 (A) Because the stems of this species stand upright, they will invariably grow too long. Therefore, you will need to trim the stems and keep the height of your plant down. Axillary buds should sprout from the stems soon, so try to replant. If you insert a cutting from a stem with leaves attached into soil, it will easily develop roots and you can propagate a new plant.

This extremely fragrant plant is used in aromatherapy.

Members of the *Plectranthus* Genus

P. pentheri

P. amboinicus variegata

P. ernstii

Haworthia pilifera / H. obtusa

Characteristics of *H. pilifera* and *H. obtusa*

These varieties grow in the arid regions of South Africa under the shade of trees and grasses. As a result, they don't like to be grown in direct sunlight. The top sides of the leaves on these unique succulents are see-through like glass, and referred to as "leaf windows." In their natural habitat, these plants grow partway underground while the windows sit above ground for photosynthesis.

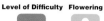

Level of Difficulty	Flowering	Native Region
★★	Spring	
Standard	Mar.–May	South Africa

Points to Check when Buying

Avoid etiolated plants whose green color is too pale and that are too tall and stretched out. Look to see if the leaves are properly glossy and plump.

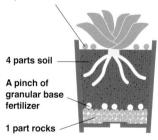

The plant should not be etiolated.

The leaves should not be discolored.

Pot

Soil Composition

Mix 5 parts small-grain Akadama, 3 parts Kanuma soil, and 2 parts mulch for a ratio that has good drainage, water retention, and breathability. Add a layer of gravel like large-grain Akadama or pumice to the bottom of the pot.

Sprinkle in an appropriate amount of granular fertilizer. You can also use liquid fertilizer.

4 parts soil

A pinch of granular base fertilizer

1 part rocks

Fertilizer

When you transplant a succulent, add a layer of granular base fertilizer on top of the layer of gravel.

How to Transplant

Pull out the seedling and remove any darkened, withered roots. Pour in new soil, spread the roots apart, and plant the succulent. Start watering after the plant has spent 4–5 days in partial shade.

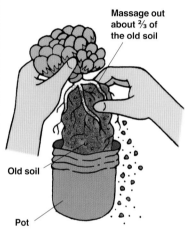

Massage out about ⅔ of the old soil

Old soil

Pot

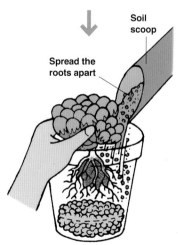

Soil scoop

Spread the roots apart

Pour in the slightly dampened new soil. When you have finished transplanting, lightly tap the pot to level the soil and place the plant in partial shade to take root.

How to Propagate

You can propagate these succulents through leaf cuttings, stem cuttings, or division. To use a leaf cutting, move the stem left and right and carefully remove a leaf. Then, let the cut end of the leaf dry before inserting it into soil.

Leaf Cutting

Let the leaf you removed from the mother plant dry for about a week, then insert it into damp soil. It will soon take root and sprout, so raise it that way until it grows large.

Division

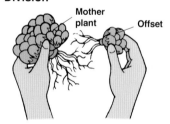

Mother plant

Offset

When an offset grows on the side of the mother plant, cut it off.

Offset

Plant the offset in fresh soil.

Key Points for Growing *H. pilifera* and *H. obtusa*

In the wild, these plants grow at the bases of bushes and trees, so grow them in partial shade and out of direct sunlight. You can use 50% shade netting to soften the sunlight, but if you shade a plant too much it will become etiolated. When the sunlight is at its strongest during midsummer, you will need shade netting of 80% or higher. These varieties hate the heat and high humidity of summer, so make sure your plant has good ventilation and water it less frequently. During the growth periods, give your plant lots of water after the soil has dried.

Cultivation Calendar

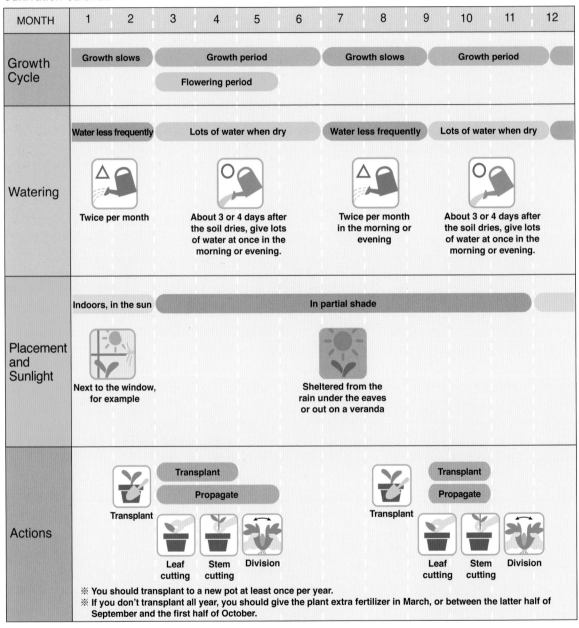

MONTH	1	2	3	4	5	6	7	8	9	10	11	12

Growth Cycle
- Growth slows (months 1–2)
- Growth period (months 3–6)
- Growth slows (months 7–8)
- Growth period (months 9–12)
- Flowering period (months 3–5)

Watering
- Water less frequently — Twice per month
- Lots of water when dry — About 3 or 4 days after the soil dries, give lots of water at once in the morning or evening.
- Water less frequently — Twice per month in the morning or evening
- Lots of water when dry — About 3 or 4 days after the soil dries, give lots of water at once in the morning or evening.

Placement and Sunlight
- Indoors, in the sun — Next to the window, for example
- In partial shade — Sheltered from the rain under the eaves or out on a veranda

Actions
- Transplant
- Propagate
- Transplant
- Leaf cutting / Stem cutting / Division
- Transplant
- Propagate
- Transplant
- Leaf cutting / Stem cutting / Division

※ You should transplant to a new pot at least once per year.
※ If you don't transplant all year, you should give the plant extra fertilizer in March, or between the latter half of September and the first half of October.

Succulent Advice Q&A

Q I placed my plant in the sun and it turned red. I don't know what to do!

A *Haworthia* plants live in partially shady environments, so if your succulent is exposed to strong, direct sunlight, it will turn red. Consider it impossible to grow your succulent out in the sun. If you put up something like shade netting (cheesecloth) and grow your plant in partial shade, it should gradually lose its redness and return to normal.

H. pilifera

H. obtusa

These varieties prefer sunlight filtering through trees over blinding, direct sun. These are curious plants that take in that sunlight through the "windows" on their leaves.

Members of the *Haworthia* Genus

H. tortuosa variegata

H. cooperi variegata

H. comptoniana

H. odetteae

H. truncata ※ Sensitive to the heat and high humidity of summer

H. truncata maughanii ※ Sensitive to the heat and high humidity of summer

55

Orostachys boehmeri

O. boehmeri

This small succulent has thinner leaves and an adorable rosette shape. Runners actively grow from the plant during the growth seasons, and the ends of the runners produce offsets so the plant can multiply and spread across the ground like a mat. *O. boehmeri* is sensitive to the heat and high humidity of summer, and its growth will stop completely in winter when its surrounding leaves wither and curl. Members of this genus originate from Japan and other parts of Asia.

Level of Difficulty	Flowering	Native Region
Easy	Sep.–Oct.	Japan

 Points to Check when Buying

Choose a plant that is full of life and energy. Check its color and luster, and make sure it has a lot of leaves and offsets.

The plant should not be etiolated. The leaves should not be discolored.

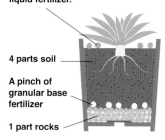

Pot

Soil Composition

Mix 5 parts small-grain Akadama, 3 parts Kanuma soil, and 2 parts mulch for a ratio that has good drainage, water retention, and breathability. Add a layer of gravel like large-grain Akadama or pumice to the bottom of the pot.

Sprinkle in an appropriate amount of granular fertilizer. You can also use liquid fertilizer.

4 parts soil

A pinch of granular base fertilizer

1 part rocks

Fertilizer

When you transplant a succulent, add a layer of granular base fertilizer on top of the layer of gravel.

How to Transplant

If you neglect to change pots for several years, the succulent will become root bound, grow weak, and die. Pull the plant from its pot, carefully massage out the old soil, and transplant in fresh soil.

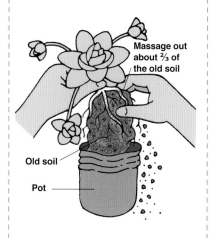

Massage out about ⅔ of the old soil

Old soil

Pot

Soil scoop

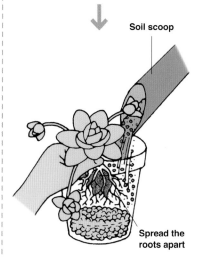

Spread the roots apart

Pour in the slightly dampened new soil. When you have finished transplanting, lightly tap the pot to level the soil and place the plant in partial shade to take root.

How to Propagate

When your plant has multiplied and filled its pot, use division. Alternatively, when offsets grow at the ends of the slender branching runners, you can cut a runner in the middle and plant it as a cutting.

Division

Mother plant

Mother plant

Runner

Offset

Divide your multiplied plants.

Place your separated plant in damp soil.

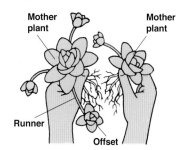

Stem Cutting

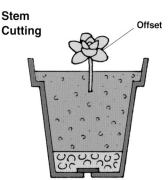

Offset

Cut off a runner with scissors or a utility knife, then insert it into soil.

57

Key Points for Growing *O. boehmeri*

This species grows naturally in rocky areas, and can even sprout in thatched roofs, although you don't see that too often anymore. Places with good drainage and ventilation are most suitable for growing these succulents. During the growing periods, you should give your plant lots of water after the soil in the pot dries out. Your succulent will be prone to rotting in summer due to the heat and high humidity, and it will stop growing in winter even though it is strong against the cold, so in these seasons you should move your plant to partial shade and be conservative when watering it.

Cultivation Calendar

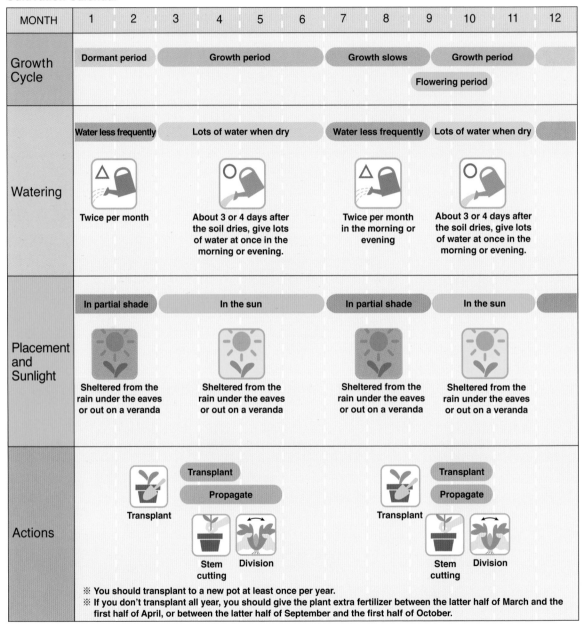

※ You should transplant to a new pot at least once per year.
※ If you don't transplant all year, you should give the plant extra fertilizer between the latter half of March and the first half of April, or between the latter half of September and the first half of October.

Succulent Advice Q&A

Q In winter, the surrounding leaves of my plant have turned brown and withered. Should I be concerned?

A This species is extremely strong against the cold and won't die even if frozen. In its dormant winter state, the lower leaves will wither, so there is nothing to worry about. If you water your plant from the middle to the end of February, it will begin to sprout in March. This may happen a month later in cold regions, but wait for the sprouting to inform you of the plant's spring awakening.

When the weather turns warm, many runners will stretch out from this plant.

Members of the *Orostachys* Genus

O. malacophylla iwarenge variegata "Fuji" ※ Sensitive to the heat and high humidity of summer

O. malacophylla iwarenge "Genkai"

O. japonica

59

Spring/Fall Types

Tillandsia harrisii (**air plants**)

Characteristics of *T. harrisii*

T. harrisii and other species of *Tillandsia* are also known as "air plants" because they absorb water from the air around them. While air plants are not technically succulents, they have come to be loved by succulent enthusiasts because they inhabit similar arid regions. They are easy to grow, even indoors, and are very popular as houseplants. Air plants grow on the surface of trees and rocks in the wild.

Level of Difficulty	Flowering	Native Region
★	✿	🗺
Easy	Varies	South America

Points to Check when Buying

Check that the leaves are not wilting and discolored and that the base is not rotting.

The leaves should not be discolored.

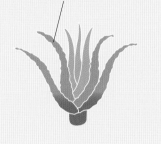

Soil Composition

Because you fundamentally do not use soil, you can grow your plants not only in common sphagnum moss, but also on a variety of materials including wood and cork, tree fern boards, and porcelain.

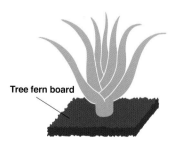

Tree fern board

Fertilizer

When you water your air plant in spring and fall, use a 1/2000 dilution of Hyponex liquid fertilizer in a bucket of water.

How to Transplant

If you are using sphagnum moss, wrap the base of the plant with moss, secure it with thread or wire, and insert the plant into its pot or other container. If you are using a slab of wood or stone, secure the plant with adhesive.

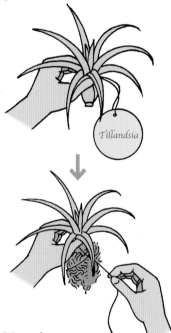

Tillandsia

Wrap sphagnum moss around the base of the plant, and then wind thread or wire around the moss to secure it.

Place your finished product into a pot, glass or tin container, or other holder, and enjoy.

How to Propagate

When an offset develops on the side of your plant after the flowering season, don't remove it right away. Wait for the offset to grow to a good size, then remove it from the mother and plant it.

Division

Mother plant   **Offset**

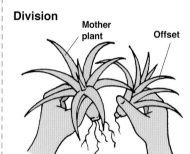

When an offset grows on the side of the mother plant, break it off by hand.

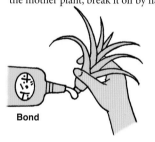

Bond

Apply Bond woodworking adhesive to the bottom of the offset.

Affix your plant to a piece of wood, cork, or porcelain.

Key Points for Growing *T. harrisii*

Instead of using soil, you can wrap sphagnum moss around the base of the plant, or adhere the plant to materials like Styrofoam or boards of cork or tree fern. In the spring and fall, give water twice a week by using a plant mister to wet the entire plant. In addition, soak your plant for 2–3 minutes once a month in a bucket or bowl filled with the dilution of liquid fertilizer in water. It should be sufficient to spray water only once per month during the humid summer when the plant's growth slows, and once every two weeks during the winter.

Cultivation Calendar

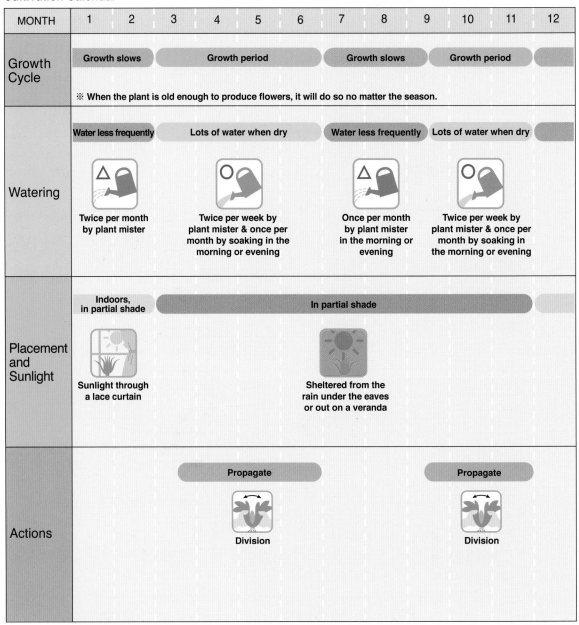

MONTH	1	2	3	4	5	6	7	8	9	10	11	12
Growth Cycle	Growth slows		Growth period				Growth slows		Growth period			

※ When the plant is old enough to produce flowers, it will do so no matter the season.

Watering

Water less frequently — Twice per month by plant mister

Lots of water when dry — Twice per week by plant mister & once per month by soaking in the morning or evening

Water less frequently — Once per month by plant mister in the morning or evening

Lots of water when dry — Twice per week by plant mister & once per month by soaking in the morning or evening

Placement and Sunlight

Indoors, in partial shade — Sunlight through a lace curtain

In partial shade — Sheltered from the rain under the eaves or out on a veranda

Actions

Propagate — Division

Propagate — Division

Succulent Advice Q&A

Q The base of my plant turned black during the summer.

A This plant does poorly in persistent high humidity. It's possible that the base of the plant stayed too moist from overwatering and rotted. Stop watering immediately and let the plant dry out in the cool shade for about half a month. Then, check the base of the plant by touching it. If the base feels soft and swollen, and if the dark discoloration has spread all the way to the leaves, then unfortunately the plant will not recover.

Flowering *T. harrisii*

This species produces beautiful flowers just by absorbing the water in the air.

Members of the *Tillandsia* Genus

T. ionantha

T. stricta

T. caput medusae

T. aeranthos

T. tricolor

T. bulbosa

CACTUS
Gymnocalycium mihanovichii "Moon Cactus" or
"Hibotan"

Characteristics of Moon Cactus

The Moon Cactus is a cultivar born from the seedlings of *G. mihanovichii* "Botandama" cacti. It was originally created in Japan, and now has become popular around the world. This cute and colorful cactus comes in a variety of hues, including red, pink, and yellow. Because this cultivar doesn't contain chlorophyll, you can't grow it unless you graft it on to another cactus. Be careful not to overexpose the cactus to direct sunlight, or the plant will sunburn, and give the plant water after the soil has dried.

Level of Difficulty — ★ Easy
Flowering — Spring Apr.–May
Native Region — Japan

Points to Check when Buying

Select a Moon Cactus that isn't etiolated, and where both the stock cactus and cultivar on top are full of energy. In particular, the stock should be green and firm.

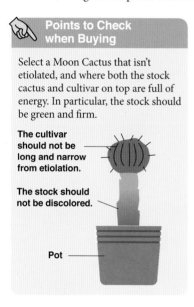

The cultivar should not be long and narrow from etiolation.

The stock should not be discolored.

Pot

Soil Composition

Mix 5 parts small-grain Akadama, 3 parts Kanuma soil, and 2 parts mulch for a ratio that has good drainage, water retention, and breathability. Add a layer of gravel like large-grain Akadama or pumice to the bottom of the pot.

Sprinkle in an appropriate amount of granular fertilizer. You can also use liquid fertilizer.

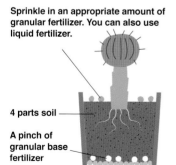

4 parts soil

A pinch of granular base fertilizer

1 part rocks

Fertilizer

When you transplant a cactus, add a layer of granular base fertilizer on top of the layer of gravel.

How to Transplant

As the plant grows, its roots will grow to fill the pot and it will become root bound, so you should remove the old soil from the roots, spread the roots apart, and pour in fresh soil. Transplant your cactus every spring.

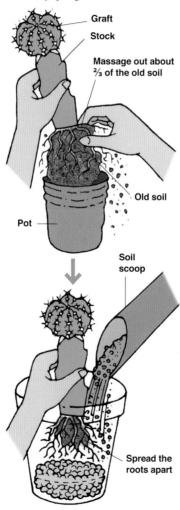

Graft

Stock

Massage out about ⅔ of the old soil

Old soil

Pot

Soil scoop

Spread the roots apart

Pour in the slightly dampened new soil. When you have finished transplanting, lightly tap the pot to level the soil and place the plant in partial shade to take root.

How to Propagate

Many offsets will develop on the side of the Moon Cactus as it grows, so cut them off and graft them to propagate the plant. For stock, use *Hylocereus undatus*, as shown in the diagram, or *Myrtillocactus geometrizans*.

Grafting

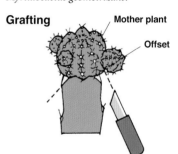

Mother plant

Offset

When an offset develops and grows large on the side of the mother plant, cut it off with a utility knife or similar tool.

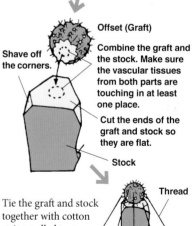

Offset (Graft)

Shave off the corners.

Combine the graft and the stock. Make sure the vascular tissues from both parts are touching in at least one place.

Cut the ends of the graft and stock so they are flat.

Stock

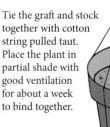

Thread

Tie the graft and stock together with cotton string pulled taut. Place the plant in partial shade with good ventilation for about a week to bind together.

65

Key Points for Growing Moon Cactus

The splendidly colored Moon Cactus grows by taking nutrients from the stock plant, so the health of the stock is critical. The stock cactus should be a robust species so it will be easy to grow. For example, the Moon Cacti that are sold in plant nurseries mainly use *Hylocereus undatus* as stock. This is an extremely hardy species, so even if you just use your intuition and give it lots of water when the soil is dry, your stock cactus should grow just fine.

Cultivation Calendar

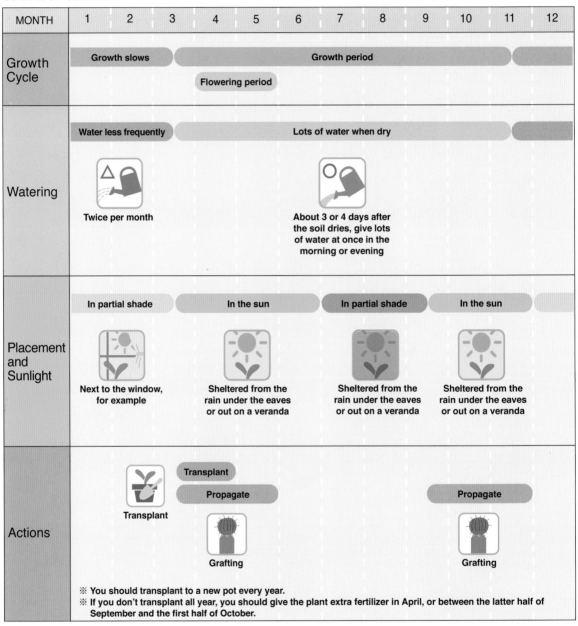

MONTH	1	2	3	4	5	6	7	8	9	10	11	12
Growth Cycle	Growth slows			Growth period								
				Flowering period								
Watering	Water less frequently			Lots of water when dry								
	Twice per month			About 3 or 4 days after the soil dries, give lots of water at once in the morning or evening								
Placement and Sunlight	In partial shade		In the sun			In partial shade			In the sun			
	Next to the window, for example		Sheltered from the rain under the eaves or out on a veranda			Sheltered from the rain under the eaves or out on a veranda			Sheltered from the rain under the eaves or out on a veranda			
Actions	Transplant		Transplant							Propagate		
			Propagate							Grafting		
			Grafting									

※ You should transplant to a new pot every year.
※ If you don't transplant all year, you should give the plant extra fertilizer in April, or between the latter half of September and the first half of October.

Succulent Advice Q&A

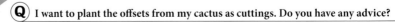

Q I want to plant the offsets from my cactus as cuttings. Do you have any advice?

A An offset will not grow if you plant it like a cutting. This cultivar doesn't contain chlorophyll and can't photosynthesize, so it must be grafted onto another cactus or "stock." When grafting, it is important to set the vascular tissue of the offset on top of that of the stock. The cells in the cut cross-section of the plant are weak, so be careful not to rub the graft and stock together.

In addition to red and yellow, the Moon Cactus can be seen in vivid pink and orange hues.

This cultivar does not contain chlorophyll, so grow it by grafting it to a green stock plant.

Members of the *Gymnocalycium* Genus

G. calochlorum

G. saglionis

G. bruchii

CACTUS

Mammillaria carmenae / Epithelantha micromeris ungnispina
"Kaguya Hime"

Characteristics of *M. carmenae* and Kaguya Hime

Compared to other cacti, these two species have an adorable little shape and relatively soft spines, so they've garnered popularity even outside of the usual cacti enthusiasts. These cacti produce offsets and grow in clusters, but because their native region of Mexico has such a harsh environment, you rarely see large clusters in the wild. They awaken early in spring and produce lots of little flowers.

Level of Difficulty	Flowering	Native Region
★	Spring	
Easy	Feb.–Apr.	Mexico

Points to Check when Buying

If the end of the cactus is pale green and tapers to a point, this is a sign of a sunlight deficiency. Also check that the cactus is not unstable to the touch.

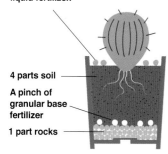

The plant should not be etiolated.

Pot

Soil Composition

Mix 5 parts small-grain Akadama, 3 parts Kanuma soil, and 2 parts mulch for a ratio that has good drainage, water retention, and breathability. Add a layer of gravel like large-grain Akadama or pumice to the bottom of the pot.

Sprinkle in an appropriate amount of granular fertilizer. You can also use liquid fertilizer.

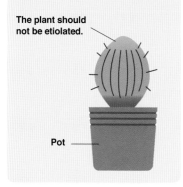

4 parts soil

A pinch of granular base fertilizer

1 part rocks

Fertilizer

When you transplant a cactus, add a layer of granular base fertilizer on top of the layer of gravel.

How to Transplant

You can transplant your cactus in spring, but if you want it to produce flowers, transplanting in early fall would be best. If the roots have spread inside the pot and the plant has become root bound, massage out the old soil, spread the roots apart, and pour in fresh soil.

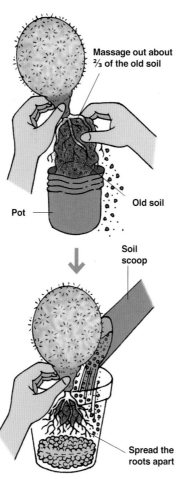

Massage out about ⅔ of the old soil

Pot

Old soil

Soil scoop

Spread the roots apart

Pour in the slightly dampened new soil. When you have finished transplanting, lightly tap the pot to level the soil and place the plant in partial shade to take root.

How to Propagate

Offsets will grow on the side of the mother plant. When the offsets grow large enough, cut them off and let the cut area dry out before planting them.

Stem Cutting

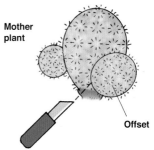

Mother plant

Offset

When an offset develops and grows large on the side of the mother plant, cut it off with a utility knife or similar tool.

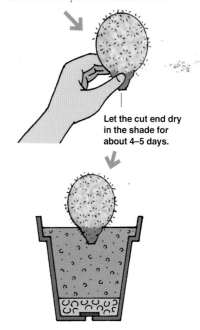

Let the cut end dry in the shade for about 4–5 days.

Place the cutting in damp soil after the cut end has dried, and in about 10 days it should take root.

Key Points for Growing *M. carmenae* and Kaguya Hime

Many varieties in these genera are robust and easy to grow. Particularly during the growth seasons of spring and fall, check for when the top soil of your plant dries out, and then give the plant lots of water about 3–4 days later. Growth will slow down in midsummer, so water the cactus less frequently and keep it in well-ventilated partial shade for the rest of the summer to prevent sunburn. These cacti are strong against the cold, and will even start to bud in the middle of winter.

Cultivation Calendar

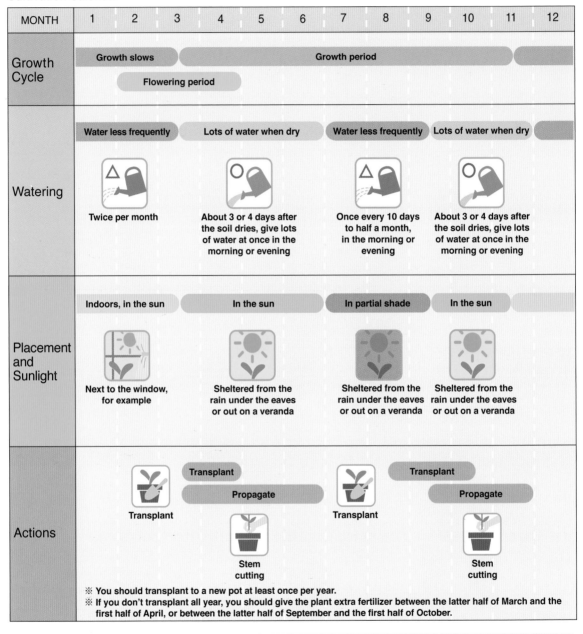

MONTH	1	2	3	4	5	6	7	8	9	10	11	12

Growth Cycle
Growth slows — Growth period
Flowering period

Watering
Water less frequently | Lots of water when dry | Water less frequently | Lots of water when dry
- Twice per month
- About 3 or 4 days after the soil dries, give lots of water at once in the morning or evening
- Once every 10 days to half a month, in the morning or evening
- About 3 or 4 days after the soil dries, give lots of water at once in the morning or evening

Placement and Sunlight
Indoors, in the sun | In the sun | In partial shade | In the sun
- Next to the window, for example
- Sheltered from the rain under the eaves or out on a veranda
- Sheltered from the rain under the eaves or out on a veranda
- Sheltered from the rain under the eaves or out on a veranda

Actions
Transplant / Propagate / Stem cutting — Transplant / Propagate / Stem cutting
- Transplant
- Transplant

※ You should transplant to a new pot at least once per year.
※ If you don't transplant all year, you should give the plant extra fertilizer between the latter half of March and the first half of April, or between the latter half of September and the first half of October.

Succulent Advice Q&A

Q Do you have any tips for making multiple flowers bloom around my cactus at once, like a crown?

A Let your plant soak in a lot of sunlight not only during the growing season, but during winter as well. When you transplant your plant during summer to free it from its root bound condition, one key point to help it produce flowers is to spread the roots apart in the new soil so that the globes can absorb more nutrients. These cacti do poorly in heat and high humidity, so find an area with good air circulation and ensure that your cactus has proper ventilation.

It's difficult to wait until spring to see the lovely flowers bloom!

Mammillaria carmenae

Epithelantha micromeris ungnispina "Princess Kaguya"

Mammillaria gracilis

Members of the *Mammillaria* Genus

M. herrerae

M. elongata "Pink Nymph"

M. prolifera multiceps

M. longimamma

M. bucareliensis "Erusamu"

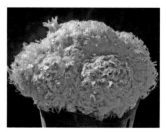

M. plumosa

Euphorbia enopla / E. mammillaris variegata "Shirakaba Kirin"

Characteristics of *E. enopla* and Shirakaba Kirin

These plants are often mistaken for cacti because they are covered in what appear to be spines, but they are actually members of the completely separate *Euphorbiaceae* family. As you get closer to the top of an *E. enopla* plant, the spines become a brilliant shade of crimson. The second species listed, known in Japan as "Shirakaba Kirin," appears to be a variegated form of *E.* "Kikkou Kirin" or *E.* "Rinpou."

Level of Difficulty	Flowering	Native Region
★	Spring	
Easy	May–Jul.	Africa

Points to Check when Buying

Plants that have grown long and narrow and taper to a point at the end are etiolated. Discolored, unsteady seedlings may have damaged roots.

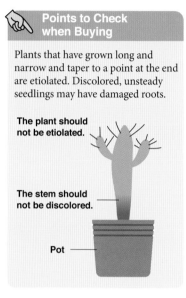

The plant should not be etiolated.

The stem should not be discolored.

Pot

Soil Composition

Mix a ratio of 5 parts small-grain Akadama, 3 parts Kanuma soil, and 2 parts mulch into a soil that has good drainage, water retention, and breathability. Add a layer of gravel like large-grain Akadama or pumice to the bottom of the pot.

Sprinkle in an appropriate amount of granular fertilizer. You can also use liquid fertilizer.

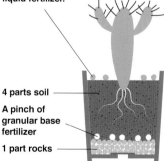

4 parts soil

A pinch of granular base fertilizer

1 part rocks

Fertilizer

When you transplant a succulent, add a layer of granular base fertilizer on top of the layer of gravel.

How to Transplant

Transplant during spring. Remove any rotten roots and massage the old soil out of the remaining roots. Look for white sap as a sign the plant is healthy, then let the plant dry for a few days before spreading the roots apart and pouring in fresh soil.

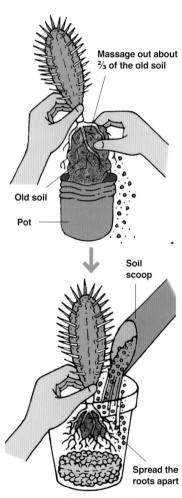

Massage out about ⅔ of the old soil

Old soil

Pot

Soil scoop

Spread the roots apart

Pour in the slightly dampened new soil. When you have finished transplanting, lightly tap the pot to level the soil and place the plant in partial shade to take root.

How to Propagate

When an offset has developed on the side of the mother plant and has grown large enough, cut it off from the base. If sap comes out, lightly wash it away with water, then let the cut end of the offset dry in the shade for about a week before inserting the cutting into soil.

Stem Cutting

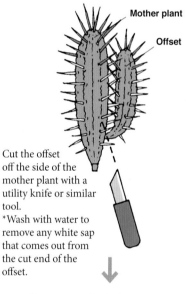

Mother plant

Offset

Cut the offset off the side of the mother plant with a utility knife or similar tool.
*Wash with water to remove any white sap that comes out from the cut end of the offset.

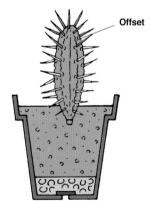

Offset

Let the cut end dry out for about a week in the shade, then plant it in damp soil.

Key Points for Growing *E. enopla* and Shirakaba Kirin

Both are relatively robust and easy to grow. They prefer hot seasons, so spring is the best time to transplant. While your seedling is still small, transplant it every year to help it grow more quickly. Overwatering these succulents leads to root rot, so it is vital that you only water after the soil is dry. Although these plants like hot weather, they don't handle high humidity well, so be careful when watering them in midsummer.

Cultivation Calendar

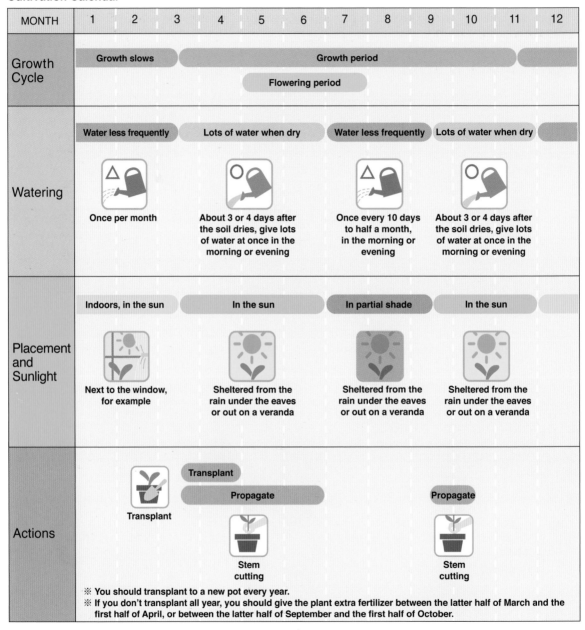

MONTH	1	2	3	4	5	6	7	8	9	10	11	12
Growth Cycle	Growth slows			Growth period								
				Flowering period								
Watering	Water less frequently			Lots of water when dry			Water less frequently			Lots of water when dry		
	Once per month			About 3 or 4 days after the soil dries, give lots of water at once in the morning or evening			Once every 10 days to half a month, in the morning or evening			About 3 or 4 days after the soil dries, give lots of water at once in the morning or evening		
Placement and Sunlight	Indoors, in the sun			In the sun			In partial shade			In the sun		
	Next to the window, for example			Sheltered from the rain under the eaves or out on a veranda			Sheltered from the rain under the eaves or out on a veranda			Sheltered from the rain under the eaves or out on a veranda		
Actions	Transplant	Transplant										
		Propagate							Propagate			
				Stem cutting						Stem cutting		

※ You should transplant to a new pot every year.
※ If you don't transplant all year, you should give the plant extra fertilizer between the latter half of March and the first half of April, or between the latter half of September and the first half of October.

Succulent Advice Q&A

Q I want to plant a cutting, but the cut end is oozing sap. How should I deal with this?

A Depending on the species of plant, the sap that comes out when you cut off a branch can be toxic and cause a skin rash. When you handle a cutting, wear gloves instead of using your bare hands and be careful not to get any sap in your mouth. Wash off the end of your cutting, taking care not to touch the sap with your bare hands.

Euphorbia enopla

Shirakaba Kirin

What appear to be spines are actually the remaining parts of flower-bearing stems called peduncles.

Members of the *Euphorbia* Genus

E. horrida

E. cylindrifolia

E. inermis

E. "Sotetsu Kirin"

E. primulifolia

E. geroldii

Agave victoriae-reginae "Hime Sasanoyuki"

Characteristics of Hime Sasanoyuki

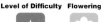
While some species in the *Agave* genus can grow up to 10 feet (3 meters) or more, Hime Sasanoyuki ranks among the smallest of these plants with a diameter of only 4 inches (10 cm). These hardy plants are strong against both the heat and the cold, and are easy to grow. They are stemless and grow pointed leaves to form a rosette. In their natural habitat, these plants grow in gravel or in crevices in boulders where drainage is good.

Level of Difficulty	Flowering	Native Region
★	Spring	
Easy	Apr.–May	Mexico

Points to Check when Buying

Select short, compact seedlings with dark green leaves. Avoid ones where the lower leaves are brown and withered.

The plant should not be etiolated and the leaves should not be discolored.

Pot

Soil Composition

Mix 5 parts small-grain Akadama, 3 parts Kanuma soil, and 2 parts mulch for a ratio that has good drainage, water retention, and breathability. Add a layer of gravel like large-grain Akadama or pumice to the bottom of the pot.

Sprinkle in an appropriate amount of granular fertilizer. You can also use liquid fertilizer.

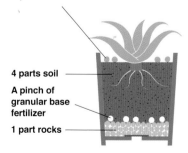

4 parts soil

A pinch of granular base fertilizer

1 part rocks

Fertilizer

When you transplant a succulent, add a layer of granular base fertilizer on top of the layer of gravel.

How to Transplant

Pull the plant from its pot, remove the old soil while taking care not to injure the roots, and move the plant to fresh soil. Leave the plant in partial shade for about 10 days before resuming normal watering.

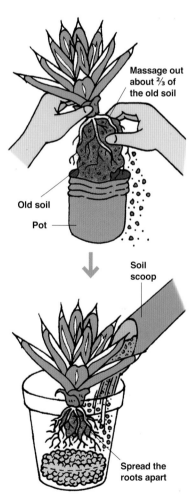

Massage out about ⅔ of the old soil

Old soil

Pot

Soil scoop

Spread the roots apart

Pour in the slightly dampened new soil. When you have finished transplanting, lightly tap the pot to level the soil and place the plant in partial shade to take root.

How to Propagate

When an offset has developed on the side of the mother plant and has grown large enough, cut it off from the base. If sap comes out, lightly wash it away with water, then let the cut end of the offset dry in the shade for about a week before inserting the cutting into soil.

Division

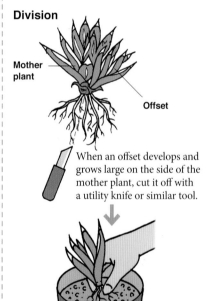

Mother plant

Offset

When an offset develops and grows large on the side of the mother plant, cut it off with a utility knife or similar tool.

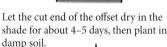

Let the cut end of the offset dry in the shade for about 4–5 days, then plant in damp soil.

※ If you plant an offset without roots in the same manner, it will take root in about 10 days.

Key Points for Growing Hime Sasanoyuki

Hime Sasanoyuki plants love the sun, and they coexist with cacti in their natural habitat. They are robust and can handle being exposed to rain during their growing periods of spring through fall; however, if the rain continues over a long period of time or if you overwater in midsummer, the moisture could lead to root rot, so move your plant under the eaves and water it less frequently. They are strong against the cold but don't grow much during the winter, so you should still water your plant less frequently during that time.

Cultivation Calendar

MONTH	1	2	3	4	5	6	7	8	9	10	11	12

Growth Cycle

Growth slows — Growth period

Flowering period

Watering

Water less frequently — Twice per month

Lots of water when dry — About 3 or 4 days after the soil dries, give lots of water at once in the morning or evening

Water less frequently — Once every 10 days to half a month, in the morning or evening

Lots of water when dry — About 3 or 4 days after the soil dries, give lots of water at once in the morning or evening

Placement and Sunlight

Indoors, in the sun — Next to the window, for example

In the sun — Sheltered from the rain under the eaves or out on a veranda

In partial shade — Sheltered from the rain under the eaves or out on a veranda

In the sun — Sheltered from the rain under the eaves or out on a veranda

Actions

Transplant
Propagate
Transplant
Division

Transplant
Propagate
Transplant
Division

※ You should transplant to a new pot at least once per year.
※ If you don't transplant all year, you should give the plant extra fertilizer in April or September.

Succulent Advice Q&A **Q** Why isn't my plant growing bigger?

A This type of Agave is slow-growing, so give your plant all the time it needs. However, if you don't transplant for a few years, the roots will grow to be tightly packed in the pot and your plant will become root bound. This will hinder your plant's development, so transplant it to encourage its growth, but be gentle so as not to injure the roots because these succulents don't like to be transplanted.

Hime Sasanoyuki's Japanese name literally means "Snow on Hime Sasa" (*Sedum lineare variegata*), and comes from the plant's striking markings reminiscent of lingering snow on the slender leaves of the Hime Sasa plant.

Members of the *Agave* Genus

A. potatorum "Raijin"

A. utahensis ※ Sensitive to the heat and high humidity of summer

A. parryi "Merico Nishiki"

A. filifera "Pinky"

A. potatorum "Ouhi-Raijin"

A. titanota variegata

Dudleya brittonii

Characteristics of *D. brittonii*

This species grows in a rosette like *Echeveria*, and flourishes along the Pacific Coast from southern California to northern Mexico. Perhaps because these plants live in dry regions with strong sunlight, their leaves are especially white. When growing *D. brittonii*, remember that they cannot handle heat and high humidity, and will grow weaker as the temperature grows hotter. If you touch the white leaves, the powder will rub off and the leaves will lose their pristine beauty.

Level of Difficulty	Flowering	Native Region
★★★ Difficult	Spring Mar.–Apr.	Mexico

Points to Check when Buying

Select a pure white plant and pass over ones where the powder has rubbed off. Select a plant that is short and compact.

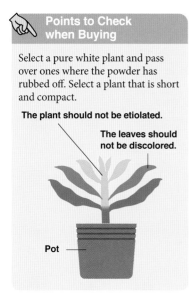

The plant should not be etiolated.

The leaves should not be discolored.

Pot

Soil Composition

Mix 5 parts small-grain Akadama, 3 parts Kanuma soil, and 2 parts mulch for a ratio that has good drainage, water retention, and breathability. Add a layer of gravel like large-grain Akadama or pumice to the bottom of the pot.

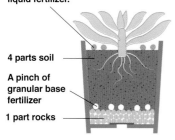

Sprinkle in an appropriate amount of granular fertilizer. You can also use liquid fertilizer.

4 parts soil

A pinch of granular base fertilizer

1 part rocks

Fertilizer

When you transplant a succulent, add a layer of granular base fertilizer on top of the layer of gravel.

How to Transplant

The best time for transplanting is early fall. Holding the plant by the stem to avoid rubbing off the white powder, remove the old soil, spread the roots apart, and pour in slightly dampened fresh soil. Leave it in partial shade, and it will take root in about 10 days.

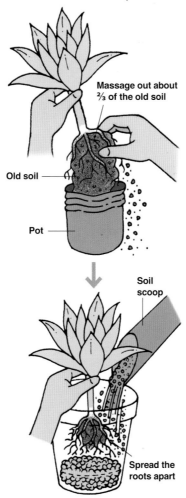

Massage out about ⅔ of the old soil

Old soil

Pot

Soil scoop

Spread the roots apart

Pour in the slightly dampened new soil. When you have finished transplanting, lightly tap the pot to level the soil and place the plant in partial shade to take root.

How to Propagate

If you have a side branch on the mother plant, cut it off, let the cut end dry for about a week, and plant the branch as a cutting. *D. brittonii* rarely produces branches, so you can propagate from seeds as well.

Seeds

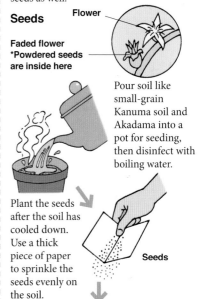

Flower

Faded flower *Powdered seeds are inside here

Pour soil like small-grain Kanuma soil and Akadama into a pot for seeding, then disinfect with boiling water.

Plant the seeds after the soil has cooled down. Use a thick piece of paper to sprinkle the seeds evenly on the soil.

Seeds

Cover the pot with something like an acrylic sheet as a lid, immerse the pot in water, and place it in the shade.

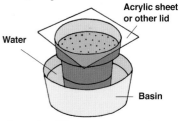

Acrylic sheet or other lid

Water

Basin

The seeds will begin to sprout in about half a month, so after they have all sprouted, remove the lid to get better air circulation and take the pot out of the standing water. Keep the soil damp, and place the pot in well-lit partial shade. Transplant a plant to a new pot when it has grown 4 or 5 leaves

Key Points for Growing *D. brittonii*

This species is sensitive to heat and high humidity, and in summer it should enter a state of semi-dormancy, so you can focus on growing these plants from fall to spring. If you have a windowsill that gets a lot of sunlight, keep your plant there during winter and continue to water it even as the temperatures drop. Flower stems will grow from the plant in early spring, but if you let all the stems produce flowers it will drain the plant's stamina, so thin some of them out. You can transplant to a new pot during spring, but it's better to do it in fall to prepare for winter.

Cultivation Calendar

MONTH	1	2	3	4	5	6	7	8	9	10	11	12
Growth Cycle	Growth slows		Growth period				Growth slows			Growth period		
			Flowering period									

Watering

Water less frequently	Lots of water when dry	Water less frequently	Lots of water when dry
Once every 10 days	About 3 or 4 days after the soil dries, give lots of water at once in the morning or evening	Twice per month in the morning or evening	About 3 or 4 days after the soil dries, give lots of water at once in the morning or evening

Placement and Sunlight

In partial shade	In the sun	In partial shade	In the sun
Next to the window, for example	Sheltered from the rain under the eaves or out on a veranda	Sheltered from the rain under the eaves or out on a veranda	Sheltered from the rain under the eaves or out on a veranda

Actions

Transplant
Transplant
Propagate
Seeds

※ You should transplant to a new pot every year.
※ If you don't transplant all year, you should give the plant extra fertilizer between the latter half of September and the first half of October.

Succulent Advice Q&A

 Q My plant started to droop as summer drew near! How can I return it to its original state?

 A This species hates summer. It originated in dry southern California, so even if it can withstand heat it struggles with high humidity. If you grow one of these plants in a place with high humidity, place it in a well-ventilated area in partial shade and be conservative when watering. To help your plant regain its energy, you must cool the plant down by moving it to a well-ventilated area and putting up black shade netting over it on a raised frame.

D. *brittonii* flowers

A fairy wearing white face powder.
If you touch her, the make-up will rub off.

Members of the *Dudleya* Genus

D. greenii "White Sprite"

D. cedrosensis

D. candida

D. pachyphytum ※ Sensitive to the
heat and high humidity of summer

D. edulis

D. lanceolate

83

Conophytum "Shukuten" / *C. obcordellum* / *C. bilobum*

Characteristics of Shukuten, *C. obcordellum,* and *C. bilobum*

Level of Difficulty	Flowering	Native Region
Standard	Fall Sep.–Nov.	South Africa

These highly evolved succulents are about ¼-⅞ inches (0.5–2 cm) in size and grow primarily in the arid regions of South Africa. Their unique, round shape is created by two leaves joining together. Their growth period is from fall to spring, and in summer they turn brown and go completely dormant. When the temperature cools again, they will break through their outer skin and begin growing. Soon after that, they will enter their flowering season. This genus has lots of other members.

 Points to Check when Buying

Select a seedling that isn't stretched too tall and narrow, and that feels firm and springy from receiving a lot of sun.

The leaves should not be discolored.

The plant should not be etiolated.

Pot

Soil Composition

Mix 5 parts small-grain Akadama, 3 parts Kanuma soil, and 2 parts mulch for a ratio that has good drainage, water retention, and breathability. Add a layer of gravel like large-grain Akadama or pumice to the bottom of the pot.

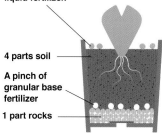

Sprinkle in an appropriate amount of granular fertilizer. You can also use liquid fertilizer.

4 parts soil

A pinch of granular base fertilizer

1 part rocks

Fertilizer

When you transplant a succulent, add a layer of granular base fertilizer on top of the layer of gravel.

How to Transplant

Pull out your plant, remove its old skin, and plant it shallowly near the surface of the soil. Massage the old soil out from its roots and add in fresh soil. Keep the soil damp, and your plant will take root in about 10 days.

Massage out about ⅔ of the old soil

Old soil

Pot

Soil scoop

Spread the roots apart

Pour in the slightly dampened new soil. When you have finished transplanting, lightly tap the pot to level the soil and place the plant in partial shade to take root.

How to Propagate

At the end of summer, propagate your plant through division or by using a cutting. Plant your new succulent near the surface of the soil, keep it slightly damp, and let it take root.

Division

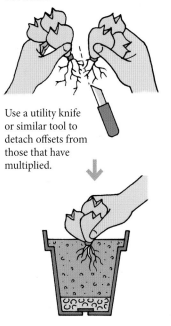

Use a utility knife or similar tool to detach offsets from those that have multiplied.

Let the detached offsets dry for 3–4 days, then plant them near the surface of the soil.

Stem Cutting

This is the stem

You can also propagate by planting an offset without any roots as a cutting. Plant the offset near the surface of the soil, about ⅜ inch (1 cm) deep.

Key Points for Growing Shukuten, *C. obcordellum*, and *C. bilobum*

The periods of growth and dormancy are clearly defined, so these succulents are easy to grow. The best time to transplant is the first week of September, right before the start of the growing period. During the growth period, it is best to refrain from frequent watering and to give lots of water after the soil dries. When the skin of the plant turns brown in early summer, this is a signal that your plant is entering dormancy, so you should mostly stop watering. Giving water at the right times is key.

Cultivation Calendar

MONTH	1	2	3	4	5	6	7	8	9	10	11	12
Growth Cycle	Growth slows		Growth gradually slows			Dormant period				Growth slows		
								Flowering period				
Watering	Lots of water when dry		Gradually begin to water less frequently		Do not water				Lots of water when dry			
			Once every 10 days to half a month, in the morning or evening						About 3 or 4 days after the soil dries, give lots of water at once in the morning or evening			
Placement and Sunlight	Indoors, in the sun	In the sun			In the shade				In the sun			
	Next to the window, for example	Sheltered from the rain under the eaves or out on a veranda			Sheltered from the rain under the eaves or out on a veranda				Sheltered from the rain under the eaves or out on a veranda			
Actions									Transplant / Propagate — Transplant; Division; Stem cutting			

※ You should transplant to a new pot every year.
※ If you don't transplant all year, you should give the plant extra fertilizer between the latter half of September and the first half of October.

Like little gems in the desert. In summer, they turn brown and fall into slumber.

Dormant *Conophytum*

Conophytum "Shukuten"

Conophytum bilobum

Conophytum obcordellum

Members of the *Conophytum* Genus

C. wittebergense

C. burgeri ※ Sensitive to the heat and high humidity of summer

C. gratum

Lithops aucampiae / L. bromfieldii insularis / L. salicola

Characteristics of *L. aucampiae, L. bromfieldii insularis,* and *L. salicola*

These highly evolved succulents can be found growing primarily in the arid regions of South Africa. They take in sunlight through the "windows" on top of their leaves for photosynthesis. These are curious plants that got their round shape from the union of two separate leaves. They are dormant during summer, and when the temperature cools they begin growing again and enter their flowering period at the same time. During the growing period, a new plant grows up from inside the old one and eventually breaks through the old skin.

Level of Difficulty	Flowering	Native Region
★★★ **Difficult**	**Fall** Sep.–Nov.	**South Africa**

Points to Check when Buying

Make sure the plant is not stretched too tall and narrow, and that the area near the base is not discolored. A short, plump plant that feels firm and springy is ideal.

The plant should not be etiolated.

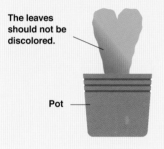

The leaves should not be discolored.

Pot

Soil Composition

Mix 5 parts small-grain Akadama, 3 parts Kanuma soil, and 2 parts mulch for a ratio that has good drainage, water retention, and breathability. Add a layer of gravel like large-grain Akadama or pumice to the bottom of the pot.

Sprinkle in an appropriate amount of granular fertilizer. You can also use liquid fertilizer.

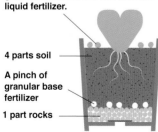

4 parts soil

A pinch of granular base fertilizer

1 part rocks

Fertilizer

When you transplant, add a layer of granular base fertilizer on top of the layer of gravel.

How to Transplant

Pull out the plant, remove its withered old skin, and plant it shallowly near the surface of the soil. To prevent root rot, be careful not to plant it in too large a pot. Remove the old soil from the roots before adding in fresh soil.

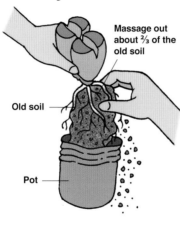

Massage out about ⅔ of the old soil

Old soil

Pot

Soil scoop

Spread the roots apart

Pour in the slightly dampened new soil. When you have finished transplanting, lightly tap the pot to level the soil and place the plant in partial shade to take root.

How to Propagate

In the beginning of fall, divide the individual offsets that have multiplied, let their cuts dry, then plant them in soil. Even if an offset doesn't have roots, as long as it has a stem, it can produce roots when planted as a cutting.

Division

Use a utility knife or similar tool to detach offsets from those that have multiplied.

Let the detached offsets dry for 3–4 days, then plant them near the surface of the soil.

Stem Cutting

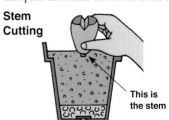

This is the stem

You can also propagate by planting an offset without any roots as a cutting. Plant the offset near the surface of the soil, about ⅜ inch (1 cm deep).

89

Key Points for Growing *L. aucampiae*, *L. bromfieldii insularis*, and *L. salicola*

Give lots of water during the growing period, every 3–4 days after the surface of the soil has dried out. If your plant remains withered even during the growth period, it may be suffering from root rot, so inspect its roots and transplant to new soil. Cease watering during summer, as this can be a cause of rot. During the dormant period, move your plant to a well-ventilated spot in the shade.

Cultivation Calendar

MONTH	1	2	3	4	5	6	7	8	9	10	11	12
Growth Cycle	Growth slows		Growth gradually slows			Dormant period				Growth slows			
									Flowering period				
Watering	Lots of water when dry		Gradually begin to water less frequently			Do not water				Lots of water when dry			
			Once every 10 days to half a month, in the morning or evening							About 3 or 4 days after the soil dries, give lots of water at once in the morning or evening				
Placement and Sunlight	Indoors, in the sun		In the sun			In the shade				In the sun			
	Next to the window, for example		Sheltered from the rain under the eaves or out on a veranda				Sheltered from the rain under the eaves or out on a veranda				Sheltered from the rain under the eaves or out on a veranda				
Actions								Transplant	Transplant / Propagate / Division / Stem cutting			

※ You should transplant to a new pot every year.
※ If you don't transplant all year, you should give the plant extra fertilizer between the latter half of September and the first half of October.

Q My plant is shedding a second layer of skin. What is the cause of this?

 A This is thought to be caused by insufficient sunlight. These plants are said to be children of the sun, so grow them in an area with a lot of sunlight exposure. Excessive watering during the growth period is also thought to be a contributing factor. Perhaps you watered the plant before the soil in the pot was sufficiently dry. Place your succulent in a well-ventilated area and be careful not to overwater.

These remarkable plants grow larger by repeatedly shedding their skins.

Lithops salicola

Lithops bromfieldii insularis

Lithops aucampiae

Lithops shedding their skins

Members of the *Lithops* Genus

L. hookeri

L. julii fulleri

L. schwantesii

Fundamentals for Growing Succulents

About Placement and Sunlight

● Placement

In places that get too much rain, succulents kept outside can retain too much moisture and develop root rot. This is a danger particularly when temperatures rise from late spring to early fall. Therefore, I recommend that you grow your plant in a place sheltered from the rain, like under the eaves or on a covered veranda.

During your plant's growth period, exposure to sunlight from morning to evening is ideal, but you can aim for three hours of sun at the least. From late spring to summer, there are succulents that grow more slowly and ones that go dormant, so during the daytime you should either block direct sunlight from your plant with cheesecloth or move it to a place in partial shade.
① Sun: A place exposed to direct sunlight.
② Partial shade: A bright place out of direct sunlight, like under the eaves. You can also weaken direct sunlight by 50% to 80% with cheesecloth (shade netting).

③ Shade: A place completely out of the sun, like the north side of your home.

● Recommendations for Cultivating in a Mini Greenhouse

It is also effective to use one of the small, portable greenhouses wrapped in clear plastic film that are sold in home and gardening stores.

<Benefits>
① The covering can keep out water, preventing the root rot that would develop during long spells of rain.
② You can cover the frame with cheesecloth to adjust the amount of sunlight coming inside.

③ The covering makes it difficult for airborne contaminants to reach the plants.
④ You can raise the temperature inside during winter days. However, the temperature inside at night will be the same as the temperature outside, so this will not prevent plants from freezing.

<Caution>
If you leave the plastic film of the greenhouse closed in the daytime during spring to fall, the inside temperature will rise, and the plants inside may sustain injuries like sunburn from the heat. Make sure to always open the film to let a breeze flow through during the day.

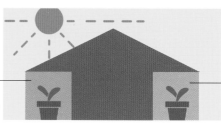

Partial shade
For example, leave your plant under the eaves facing east where it will only receive sun in the morning.

Shade
For example, leave your plant under the eaves facing north where it will not receive any sun throughout the day.

About Watering

No plant can survive without water. Even though succulents store water inside themselves, they still require a certain amount of help from the outside. To grow a healthy succulent, it's important to learn its specific needs and the best techniques for watering it.

The basic rule for watering is to give lots of water about 3–4 days after the surface of the soil has dried during the plant's growth period. Pour water into the top of the pot until it flows out the hole in the bottom. When the plant begins growing more slowly, water it less frequently, and when it goes dormant, stop watering altogether.

The "immersion method" is one way of watering. If you pour water on varieties covered in white powder from above their leaves, the powder will wash away and ruin the plant's pristine appearance. Instead, fill a container with water and immerse the whole lower part of the flowerpot, allowing the soil to absorb water through the hole in the bottom.

<Tips>
• Judge the amount of moisture in the soil from its color. (top photo)
• Even if the surface of the soil is dry, you won't know how wet the soil is deeper down, so insert a skewer into the soil and occasionally pull it out to check the level of moisture. (middle photo)
• If sunlight hits places where water is gathered between the leaves, the drops of water can act like a lens and cause sunburn. If water droplets form, blow them away with a dust blower designed for cameras. (bottom photo)

Immersion method

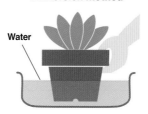

Water

The soil on the left is dry, and the soil on the right is wet.

Check the wetness of the soil inside the pot with a skewer.

Blow away drops of water with a dust blower.

About Planting Soil

People often tell me that they are unsure of which soil is best for planting succulents. Keep the following points in mind when choosing the soil most suitable for your plant.

① Drainage: The soil will quickly drain away excess water. If water is left to accumulate inside the pot indefinitely, it can lead to root rot.

② Water retention: Retaining an appropriate amount of water in the soil will stimulate growth of the roots.

③ Breathability: Roots need to breathe too, so it is essential that they can always access fresh air.

As long as you satisfy these three requirements, it won't matter what soil you use. A variety of soils are sold at home and gardening stores, so if you buy several types and combine them, you can anticipate good results from the plants you grow.

For example, one option is to use Akadama as the main component, then mix in ingredients like Kanuma soil, mulch, and carbonized rice hull to make a soil mixture. If you further sift this mixture and remove the finely powdered particles of soil, your plants will grow even better.

※ You can use Hyuga soil instead of Akadama.

HydroBalls　Mulch　Vermiculite　Carbonized rice hull

Small-grain Kanuma soil　Large-grain Akadama　Small-grain Akadama　Sphagnum moss

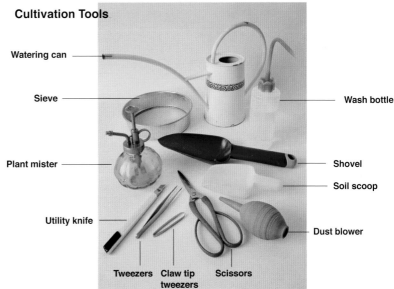

Cultivation Tools

Watering can
Sieve
Plant mister
Utility knife
Tweezers　Claw tip tweezers　Scissors
Wash bottle
Shovel
Soil scoop
Dust blower

Lasting through Summer and Winter

Watch Out for Sunburns and Root Rot

Succulents that are sensitive to heat and high humidity are liable to sunburn when the sun's rays grow strong during early to midsummer. Dampen the sunlight with cheesecloth or move your plant into partial shade where a breeze can pass through. Additionally, because your succulent's growth slows down during the summer, overwatering will lead to root rot, so give it water less frequently during this period.

Handling the Cold and Preventing Freezing

It is safer to move succulents like Kalanchoe that freeze easily to a sunny area indoors. Even plants that are comparatively strong against the cold should still be taken indoors for days there is a risk of freezing and for the low temperatures in the morning and evening. If you water less frequently during midwinter, the plant will store less water inside itself and be less likely to freeze.

Sunburned Conophytum

Frozen Kalanchoe

Glossary

Areole

The point where spines connect to a cactus.

Base Fertilizer

Fertilizer applied before potting a plant. Either add slow-release granular fertilizer on top of the bottom layer of gravel or mix it directly into the soil.

Cheesecloth/Shade Netting

A sheet woven from black or white fibers. It can block and soften direct sunlight, and is available in varieties that block 30%, 50%, or 80% of sunlight.

Chlorophyll

The pigments inside the leaves of plants. These pigments use sunlight, carbon dioxide, and water to make the carbohydrates that nourish the plant.

Crossbreeding

Pollinizing to collect seeds. You can also crossbreed two varieties together to create a new one.

Dormant Period

When the plant stops growing in the summer or winter. *Conophytum* and *Lithops* are representative genera that go dormant in summer.

Etiolation

When a plant stretches out too long and narrow due to a lack of sunlight. To return the plant to normal, remove the top part as a cutting, plant it, and grow it again from scratch.

Extra Fertilizer

Fertilizer added after a plant has already grown considerably.

Fasciation

When a plant has multiple points of growth and becomes misshapen.

Grafting

Raising a variety that is hard to cultivate by attaching it to a robust, fast-growing stock plant.

Gravel Layer

The layer of large-grain soil at the bottom of a flowerpot. Refers to materials like large-grain Akadama and pumice.

Immersion Method

To fill a container with water, place your flowerpot in the container, and let the soil absorb water through the hole in the bottom of the pot.

Irrigation

Supplying water to the soil inside the flowerpot.

Leaf Cutting

A leaf removed from a stem that can be used for propagation by being placed on top of soil to produce roots.

Liquid Fertilizer

A fast-acting, liquid version of fertilizer containing the three fertilizer components of nitrogen, phosphoric acid, and potassium. Dilute the prescribed amount with water and use the solution as extra fertilizer by pouring it in from the top of the soil.

Misting

Using a plant mister to cover a plant in water. This method of watering is suitable for *Tillandsia* plants that can absorb water through their leaves.

Mulch

Sufficiently fermented fallen leaves. It has good water retention and drainage.

Offset

A daughter plant that grows from the side of the mother plant.

Offset Propagation

To breed a new plant from an offset that was cut with a knife off the side of another plant's stem.

Organic Fertilizer

Fertilizer made from organic ingredients like compost, food dregs from oil extraction, and fish meal.

Partial Shade

A place untouched by direct sunlight, like under the gentle light filtering through the trees. You can soften the sunlight by using cheesecloth, creating partial shade.

Photosynthesis

The process by which green plants use sunlight, carbon dioxide, and water to produce glucose.

Planting Soil

Soil for raising succulent plants. Composed of ingredients with good drainage, water retention, and breathability.

Root Cutting

A thick root removed from the stem of a plant like *Haworthia* that will sprout when planted in soil and can be used for propagation.

Rosette

An arrangement of leaves to look like a round elliptical or polygon-shaped flower.

Seeding

Taking seeds from a plant after it flowers, planting them in fresh soil, and letting them sprout.

Self-pollination

When pollen from a plant attaches to the pistil of a flower from that same plant.

Shade

A place completely untouched by sunlight.

Shedding

When plants of genera like *Conophytum* and *Lithops* from the *Aizoaceae* family shed their old skin.

Slow-release Fertilizer

Fertilizer with effects that appear slowly and are long-lasting.

Softening Sunlight

Using cheesecloth or shade netting to weaken strong sunlight.

Soggy Soil

Soil that is always wet and warm. When wet soil heats up, the inside is similar to hot water and will damage the roots.

Stem Cutting

A branch or offset cut from the side of a stem that can be planted in soil to create a new plant.

Sun

A place that receives direct sunlight.

Tuber

A stem that has grown round and thick to store water.

Tuberous Root

A root that has become extremely swollen to store water.

Variegated ("Variegata")

When a plant's green leaves have areas without chlorophyll, creating patterns of other colors like white and yellow.

Ventilating

Opening the cover of your greenhouse and improving air flow so the temperature inside does not rise too high.

Watering

Pouring water into the soil, as from a watering can.

Defenses Against Diseases and Pests (※ indicates effective methods and treatments)

<Diseases>

Blight

The decay progresses from the base of the plant up the stem.
※ Copper and sulpher fungicides are helpful.

Filamentous Fungi

The soil at base of your plant will appear to be covered in threads. These fungi are a type of mold, and as the temperature rises, plants like *Lithops* are at risk of developing a fungus of this variety and rotting.
※ Prevent with Topsin M, Benlate, or Daconil.

Gray Mold

Gray-brown specks of mold develop and spoil the leaves. This mold grows easily with a lack of sunlight and poor ventilation.
※ Apply Dithane, Daconil, or Benlate.

Powdery Mildew

The surface of the leaves becomes covered in white powder. This can be caused by heat and poor ventilation.
※Apply Ortran C , Saprol EC, or a copper fungicide.

Soft Rot

If you grow a plant weakly, it will decay more easily.
※Prevent this by raising a strong plant with a lot of sunlight and good ventilation.

Sooty Mold

The leaves become dirty as if covered in soot. This fungus clings to the excrement of aphids and scale insects.
※ Apply Karphos EC, horticultural oil or neem oil.

Sunburn

When seedlings that have been weakened by a lack of sunlight are exposed to strong direct sunlight, they discolor.
※ Prevent this by weakening the sunlight with cheesecloth.

<Pests>

Aphids

Aphids multiply rapidly and weaken plants by sucking out their juices.
※ Numerous aphicides are available; a solution of water and dish soap may forestall a need for chemical treatment

Armyworms

These insects come out at night and eat the tender leaves of plants.
※ Prevent this by placing a granular insecticide on the soil.

Cottony Cushion Scale

You will notice these insects wrapped in fluffy cotton right away because they move when touched. They weaken plants by sucking out their juices.
※ Apply Karphos EC to the base of your plant. Neem oil or horticultural oil can also treat scale pests.

Red Spider Mites

These are tiny, red insects that you wouldn't notice without a magnifying glass. Spider mites suck the juices from plants, so the skin of the plants will turn brown.
※ Apply a mixture of pesticides like chlorobenzilate, Kelthane, and Amitraz.

Root Mealybugs

A white, powdery substance will be attached to the area around the plant's roots. Wash the roots with water and let them dry in the shade for a few days to eliminate the pests.
※ Prevent this by scattering granular pesticide around the base of the plant.

Scale Insects

These insects appear to wear white seashells on their backs, and weaken plants by sucking out their juices.
※ Rub the insects off with a toothbrush. Apply insecticide and let the plant absorb it.

Slugs

Slugs come out at night and eat the tender parts of plants.
※ Scatter a granular pesticide formulated for slugs on the soil.

Note: The topical and systemic treatments mentioned above include both brand-name chemicals and less hazardous treatments that are available through such companies as Bonide, Monterey and others. Other options include home remedies (dish soap, isopropyl alcohol and so on). When using any preparation or ingredients, always follow the manufacturer's directions and take appropriate steps to protect yourself from inhaling, ingesting or exposing your skin to these substances.

Published by Tuttle Publishing, an imprint of Periplus Editions (HK) Ltd. 2018

978-0-8048-5119-0

ILLUST & SHASHIN DE MIRU TANIKUSHOKUBUTSU
NO TANOSHIMIKATA TO SODATEKATA
Copyright © Taku Furuya 2016
English translation rights arranged with Nitto Shoin
Honsha Co., Ltd. through Japan UNI Agency, Inc., Tokyo
Translated from Japanese by HL Partners, LLC

Staff:
Planning and Composition / Monoart Co. Ltd.
Photography / Kazumasa Yamamoto
Provider of Illustrations and Photos / Taku Furuya
Text Design / ichimilli CreativeWorks
Cover Design / ME&MIRACO (Kana Tsukada)
Planning and Progress / Kaori Kaburagi
Research Collaboration / International Succulent
Institute of Japan;
Tokyo Cactus Club; Yokosuka Cactus Club;
Cactus Hirose Co. Ltd.
Photography Collaboration / Sekisui House, Ltd.
Yokosuka Exhibition

Distributed by:

North America, Latin America & Europe
Tuttle Publishing
364 Innovation Drive, North Clarendon
VT 05759-9436 U.S.A.
Tel: 1 (802) 773-8930; Fax: 1 (802) 773-6993
info@tuttlepublishing.com; www.tuttlepublishing.com

Japan
Tuttle Publishing
Yaekari Building 3rd Floor
5-4-12 Osaki Shinagawa-ku, Tokyo 141 0032
Tel: (81) 3 5437-0171; Fax: (81) 3 5437-0755
sales@tuttle.co.jp; www.tuttle.co.jp

Asia Pacific
Berkeley Books Pte. Ltd.
3 Kallang Sector, #04-01/02, Singapore 349278
Tel: (65) 6280-1330; Fax: (65) 6280-6290
inquiries@periplus.com.sg; www.periplus.com

Printed in Hong Kong   1810EP
22 21 20 19   10 9 8 7 6 5 4 3 2 1

About Tuttle "Books to Span the East and West"

Our core mission at Tuttle Publishing is to create books which bring people together one page at a time. Tuttle was founded in 1832 in the small New England town of Rutland, Vermont (USA). Our fundamental values remain as strong today as they were then—to publish best-in-class books informing the English-speaking world about the countries and peoples of Asia. The world has become a smaller place today and Asia's economic, cultural and political influence has expanded, yet the need for meaningful dialogue and information about this diverse region has never been greater. Since 1948, Tuttle has been a leader in publishing books on the cultures, arts, cuisines, languages and literatures of Asia. Our authors and photographers have won numerous awards and Tuttle has published thousands of books on subjects ranging from martial arts to paper crafts. We welcome you to explore the wealth of information available on Asia at **www.tuttlepublishing.com.**